Selecting an Ada®Compilation System

® Ada is a registered trademark of the Ada Joint Program Office – US Government

The Ada Companion Series

There are currently no better candidates for co-ordinated, low-risk, and synergetic approach to software development than the Ada programming language. Integrated into a support environment, Ada promises to give a solid standards-orientated foundation for higher professionalism in software engineering.

This definitive series aims to be the guide to the Ada software industry for 'managers, implementors, software producers and users. It will deal with all aspects of the emerging industry: adopting an Ada strategy, conversion issues, style and portability issues, and management. to assist the organised development of an Ada-oriented software components industry, equal emphasis will be placed on all phases of life cycle support.

Some current titles:

Ada: Languages, compilers and bibliography
Edited by M.W. Rogers

Proceedings of the 1985 Ada International Conference
Edited by J.G.P. Barnes and G.A. Fisher

Ada for specification: possibilities and limitations
Edited by S.J. Goldsack

Concurrent programming in Ada
A. Burns

Selecting an Ada environment
Edited by T.G.L. Lyons and J.C.D. Nissen

Ada components: Libraries and tools
Proceedings of the 1987 Ada-Europe International Conference
Edited by S. Tafvelin

Ada: the design choice
Proceedings of the 1989 Ada-Europe International Conference
Edited by A. Alvarez

Distributed Ada: developments and experiences
Proceedings of the Distributed Ada '89 Symposium, Southampton
Edited by J.M. Bishop

Ada: experiences and prospects
Proceedings of the 1990 Ada-Europe International Conferences
Edited by Barry Lynch

Selecting an Ada Compilation System

Edited by
J. DAWES
International Computers Ltd., UK

M.J. Pickett
Sema Group plc, UK

A. Wearing
NCC Ltd., UK

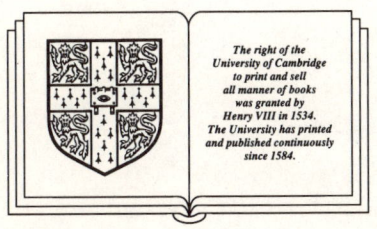

CAMBRIDGE UNIVERSITY PRESS

Cambridge
New York   Port Chester   Melbourne   Sydney

Published by the Press Syndicate of the University of Cambridge
The Pitt Building, Trumpington Street, Cambridge CB2 1RP
40 West 20th Street, New York, NY 10011, USA
10 Stamford Road, Oakleigh, Melbourne 3166, Australia

© Cambridge University Press 1990

First published 1990

Printed in Great Britain at the University Press, Cambridge

Library of Congress Cataloguing in Publication data available

British Library cataloguing in publication data available

ISBN 0 521 40498 3

CONTENTS

Foreword vii

Preface ix

Introduction 1

Part I Application Requirements

1. Introduction to Part I 7
2. Long Lifetime 9
3. Large Program Size 11
4. Portability 13
5. Compile-Time Operational Qualities 15
6. Software Interfacing 21
7. Run-Time Operational Qualities 25
8. Concurrency 31
9. Security 35
10. Timing Constraints 37
11. Host-Target Development 41
12. Embedded Application Systems 43
13. Hardware Interfacing 47
14. Exploitation of Target and Computational Capacity . . . 49
15. Multiprocessing 51
16. Use of High Level Tools 59
17. Training 61

Part II Questionnaires

18. Introduction to Part II 67
19. Compilation System Facilities 69
20. Quality and Documentation 79
21. Performance and Capacity 91
22. Run-Time Implementation Concerns 99
23. Architectural Considerations 103
24. Man-Machine Interface 127
25. Language-Related Characteristics 131
26. Tool-Building Activities 139
27. Contractual Matters 143

Part III Sources of Information

28. Introduction to Part III 153
29. Benchmarks 155
30. Evaluation Systems 159
31. Published Literature 161

Glossary 163

References 167

FOREWORD

At the time the first attempt was made to specify what criteria one should apply when selecting a compilation system (in the Ada Companion Series Volume Ada: Language, Compilers and Bibliography), the world was much simpler. At the end of 1983 there were just three compilers which implemented the full language. By May 1985 it was obvious at the Ada in Use World Conference that the outlook for Ada would take an upswing, as the procurement policies of more and more agencies adopted Ada as a standard.

1985 saw a jump from 14 to 75 compilers. By April 1989, there were 171 base compilers, and over 70 derived compilers. A compiler is the minimal compilation system possible, so now that is the selection basis from which a choice has to be made. Also, these offerings come from 50 independent vendors, complicating the information gathering process. The Compiler Validation report is one valuable constant factor however.

Ada language compilers, and thus compilation systems, will still exhibit small implementation deviations from one another. This is due to differences in interpretation of the Ada Language Reference Manual. Comparative to other languages though in the history of computing these are "minor".

It is the tools that should make a major difference in the attraction of one compilation system vis-a-vis another. Tools have direct implications in productivity terms, and deserve recognition. This book makes a clear distinction about those tools that directly support a compiler. The book makes a first attempt to explain the advantages of these tools. It considers strengths and weaknesses, as well as discussing boundary conditions under which certain characteristics, such as portability, can be ensured in a changing requirements situation often encountered in complex software systems.

For example, a recent major survey into cost estimates for software production showed an Ada specific model, together with a good compilation tool set, could predict, within 25%, real end costs 75% of the time. This is a very enviable success rate for software costs estimation models. This proves that with the choices of good production tool sets, complex software projects can be engineered and executed within reasonable commercial criteria if Ada is used.

Only the computer children of the 1960's card punch generation can realise the envy with which we read of structured cross referencers, interactive debugging, library managers etc. Run-time issues simply didn't exist for us, with an overnight turnaround! Software was just "done", not produced - and certainly not engineered. Now, in the information age of the 90's, software is a production business and we need to choose our tools very carefully.

Also, one may be inclined to say that a book such as this is invariably rapidly out of date. Having been a European representative on the Ada Board in the USA for some years, the revision process implemented for the language will take some time to complete. It will also seek to minimise the impact on the language - highlighting points of clarification and common interpretation. This ensures minimal compiler changes. Therefore compilation systems in general will also experience minimal changes if they support compilers essentially.

Like in so many other cases, Ada is as useful as a tool for articulating a problem domain as it is as a compilable language. Compilation systems tools extend the language, and thus make it an even more powerful tool. High level primitives, other than those in the language, can be encapsulated easily. Software engineering a solution to optimise the application implementation becomes feasible.

It is clear that buying a language now for an application is no longer a trivial or transparent decision. If not already imposed upon the designer, it is up to the implementor to enable the maximisation of investment by the user, and offer optimal forward compatibility, and portability to likely future systems. The developer must eradicate errors before delivery, and have a system in which security and integrity are maintained. The compiler and associated tools are the fundamental tools available, and their considered selection the single most important implementation decision in a project. Use the advice collected from many specialists and presented in this book, and you will make a state of the art decision of which you can be sure.

Mike W Rogers

PREFACE

This guide is intended to promote the effective use of Ada by providing guidance to users on:

- formulation of requirements on Ada compilation systems for particular application domains;

- evaluation of Ada compilation systems against requirements;

- selection of an Ada compilation system on the basis of the evaluation.

This guide was produced by the Ada-Europe Compilation Systems Assessment Working Group, under the chairmanship of Michael Pickett. Meetings of the Ada-Europe working group were partially funded by the Commission of the European Communities.

Production of this guide has relied extensively on voluntary effort. The contributors were John Dawes (International Computers Ltd, UK), Ted Dowling (Ferranti Computer Systems, UK), Mike Harrison (INMOS Ltd, UK), Lennart Mansson (Telelogic AB, Sweden), Michael Pickett (Sema Group plc, UK), Ron Pierce (IPSYS Software Ltd, UK), Trevor Syms (NATO, ADASCC, NICSMA), Alison Wearing (NCC Ltd, UK), Brian Wichmann (NPL, UK), and Olle Wikstrom (Ericsson Radio Systems AB, Sweden), John Dawes was secretary to the working group. John Dawes, Michael Pickett and Alison Wearing edited the book and dealt with word processing. Thanks are due to Sema Group plc, International Computers Ltd and NCC Ltd for providing the necessary facilities to enable this work to progress.

The Guide cannot ever be considered complete. As new interpretations to the Ada language are agreed and new application requirements developed, evaluation criteria will change. The editors would welcome comments on the Guide. Written comments, dated, with the author's name, address and telephone number, quoting section number if relevant, should be sent to:

Mr Michael Pickett
Sema Group plc
Orion Court
Kenavon Drive
Reading
Berkshire
RG1 3DQ
UK

Comments about Ada Compilation Systems are being collected in the Eurokom computer conferencing service. The conference, Ada Compilation System Comments, is organised by the NCC Ltd. If you wish to receive further information about the conference please contact:

Alison Wearing
NCC Ltd
Oxford Road
Manchester
M1 7ED
UK

INTRODUCTION

This Guide is concerned with selecting an Ada compilation system for a software project. If the project team is moving to Ada from a different language then there are clearly particular factors which must also be considered with the choice of compilation system to give a complete picture. The purpose of this Guide is to provide key questions and background information to give the user specific information on which to make an informed choice of compilation system.

A previous Guide (Rogers 1981) was produced which primarily considered the choice of an Ada compilation system from the viewpoint of a compiler writer. In that Guide detailed information was given about specific language features which might or might not be relevant to the user of the compilation system. This Guide addresses specifically the needs of a user of a compilation system. It is concerned more with the effects of features of the language and compilation system than with the features themselves. In the production of this Guide the previous Guide has been used as a source of information and as a checklist to ensure that the relevant issues have been considered, but the material is new, reflecting the different objectives of the two Guides.

The Language Ada

Ada is a language originally conceived for real-time and embedded system applications, such as command and control or fighter aircraft systems. However, the design of the language has made it suitable for many applications. The Reference Manual for the Ada Programming Language (ANSI/MIL-STD 1815A 1983) is published by the US Department of Defense (DoD). Ada became an ANSI standard in February 1983 and an International Standard in March 1987. The standard is jointly controlled by the Ada Joint Program Office (AJPO), part of the US DoD, and an ISO/IEC Working Group (JTC 1/SC22/WG9 Ada). At the time of writing this Guide resolution of any issues concerning interpretations of the Reference Manual requires approval by both organisations. Work began in 1988 to revise the standard for publication in the early 1990s. It has been recommended to the AJPO, the sponsors of the revision, that the objective of the proposed new standard should be to select only those changes that improve the usability of the language, for example supporting an extended character set, while minimising the disruptive effects of changing the standard.

When Ada was first launched it was unique in that the DoD registered the name as a trademark through the AJPO. The AJPO commissioned a validation test suite, and for any compiler to be legitimately named Ada it must have passed all applicable tests in the validation test suite; there is no allowance for any failures. Until the end of 1988 the compiler had to pass the validation test suite every twelve months. As new test suites were issued every twelve months this meant that the compiler was more exhaustively tested each year.

Since 1st December 1987, the AJPO has relaxed its policy on trademarking but the validation test suite remains, and retains its importance as a criterion for Ada compilation systems acceptance. From the beginning of 1989 the policy has been to issue new test suites every eighteen months. This change in policy is due to the increasing maturity of the validation test suite as fewer changes are expected. The expiration date of the validation certificate has been changed from twelve months after the date of validation to twelve months after the expiration of the corresponding test suite. A supplier can make minor adjustments to the compiler, at the supplier's discretion, within this period. However if major changes are made, for example the compiler is moved to a different operating system or new target, then revalidation is required.

The Ada Compilation System

For the purposes of this Guide, the compilation system is taken to consist of the tools which are an integral part the Ada system: editor, compiler, various listing tools, linker, target loader, and debugger. Ada Project Support Environments (APSEs) are not considered because they are the subject of a separate guide by the Ada-Europe Environment Working Group (Lyons and Nissen, 1986).

With Ada, there are likely to be several suitable development systems for any application. With many programming languages, compilers are available almost exclusively from hardware manufacturers; but with Ada independent supply is common. This makes the process of selecting a compilation system more complex. The choice of systems nevertheless increases the competitiveness of the Ada market.

Structure of the Guide

For an effective evaluation, it is essential that the nature of the application domain is understood in the Ada context; that relevant questions can be asked of suppliers of Ada compilation systems; and that for quantitative evaluation, benchmark programs can be run and the results interpreted. This pattern is reflected in the structure of the Guide.

Part I of this Guide contains a number of chapters, each discussing some salient characteristic of applications, such as large size or requirement for interfacing, and the implications for the compilation system. Part II contains questionnaires, each covering some aspect of the compilation system. For each question, guidance is given on the kinds of answers to expect and on interpreting the possible answers. Part III contains a number of chapters on various available sources of information which may be useful in obtaining answers to the questions in Part II.

There is nothing to prevent readers using the Guide in whatever way they wish, but the idea of the Guide is that readers, using their knowledge of the nature of the application, first decide, with the help of the appropriate chapters of Part I, which aspects of the Ada compilation system are significant and are so led to the appropriate questionnaires in Part II.

PART I Application Requirements

1

Introduction To Part I

This part of the Guide discusses, in general terms, how various features of the application affect requirements placed on the Ada compilation system.

As the field of application of Ada is large and growing daily, and it seems impossible to put bounds to its growth, it is not practical to discuss individual types of application; instead some general features common to various types of application have been selected. It is hoped that the list covers most if not all of the significant features and how they apply to any given application.

The features covered and their relevance are listed in table 1. The features are presented in an order in which the more general or administrative features are followed by the more specific or technical features. Each chapter stands in its own right and does not assume that the reader has read the earlier chapters. Therefore a reader may select only those chapters which are deemed to be relevant.

Table 1
Features Covered in the Guide

Feature	Relevance
Long Lifetime	Applications which must remain in service for many years
Large Program Size	Applications requiring more than a few man months of effort to develop
Portability	Applications which may be required to run in or be maintained in a variety of environments
Compile-time Operational Qualities	The development and maintenance of the application
Software Interfacing	Interfaces an application may have with other software
Run-time Operational Qualities	The impact of the compilation system on various aspects of the behaviour of the application
Concurrency	Applications in which a number of activities are progressing simultaneously
Security	The protection of information from unauthorised access
Timing Constraints	Applications for which the response in real-time may be critical
Host-Target Development System	Applications which are run on different computers from those on which they are developed
Embedded Systems	Applications where the computer is only a component of a larger system
Hardware Interfacing	Applications which need to address hardware devices directly
Exploitation of Target and Computational Capacity	The effectiveness of the compilation system in making use of the target hardware
Multi-processing	Applications running on multi-processor target computers
Use of High-Level Tools	Applications for which the source code was generated automatically
Training	The training of professional software developers in the language Ada

2

Long Lifetime

Software systems expected to remain in service for a long time are likely to place special requirements on the compilation system used to implement them. By a long lifetime is meant a total life which is many times as long as the initial development phase, and which lasts at least five years.

Even in the most stable environment a software system must be expected to be subjected to change, as enhancements are required and errors are discovered. In most cases the environment is far from stable and the system must change to keep in step. Maintainability is therefore likely to be an important consideration. There are two main aspects: maintainability of the compilation system and maintainability of the application.

2.1   Maintainability of the compilation system

The compilation system used is unlikely to be entirely stable. Ideally, the same version of the compilation system would be used throughout the life of the system, from initial development through further development and maintenance; but this is unlikely to be possible in practice. Difficulties inevitably arise as changes to the source code uncover errors in the compilation system, and it is necessary to plan to meet them. The requirement for validation of Ada compilation systems certainly helps to ensure forward compatibility, but brings its own problems:

- Old versions of compilation systems may not be revalidated. This might be because the language has effectively changed, for instance when a decision of the ISO working group overturns a previously accepted interpretation or there is a revision of the Ada standard. This might affect the status of the system under development in the eyes of the end-user.

- Similarly, even though the compilation system does not change, new versions of the operating system or other software may affect the status of the development with regard to validation. This is because validation applies to a compilation system in the context of a particular hardware and software environment.

It is important to decide what to do about these problems at the outset, and then ensure that the compilation system chosen can support the decision.

On the one hand, for stability, the compilation system must remain usable, and perhaps validated, for the lifetime of the product, though the requirement to revalidate may force changes on a compilation system. Some important considerations are the maturity of the compilation system, how much use it has had and is likely to have in the future, and any guarantees of maintenance by the supplier.

On the other hand, for controlling upgrades to new versions, it is necessary to know the supplier's intentions and commitments to producing and validating new versions, and to maintaining forward compatibility. A new version without forward compatibility may necessitate complete recompilation, which may be undesirable or even impossible, for instance if pre-compiled packages have been acquired.

Finally, it is worth taking precautions against the supplier going out of business; for instance copies of the source code and documentation of the compilation system can be held by a third party.

2.2   Maintainability of the application

The requirement to be able to produce a maintainable system is met to some extent by the use of Ada. Further assistance in meeting this requirement can be provided by compiler options and tools.

- Good documentation is required, and facilities for producing and controlling it are valuable; examples of such facilities are cross-reference listers, formatted source listers, and library managers.

- Good readable code is also required. If the code is going to remain in service a long time then it is worth ensuring that it is of good quality. Facilities can be provided to assist in achieving this.Examples are testing, debugging, and verification aids, and options in the compiler to police coding standards.

- A long-lived system goes through many changes, so that considerations of change control are important. The structure of the program library and the facilities it offers may be relevant here. The possibility that the system may change host must be considered; if the possibility exists, then portability of the application is important. See chapter 4, Portability.

3

Large Program Size

Common characteristics of large programs are: they are developed by large project teams; a high proportion of the software comprises reusable components; there are multiple Program Libraries; many recompilations are needed; many test versions and base-line versions are produced during the development phase; and the binary image is large. All these characteristics have implications for the choice of compilation system.

The method normally employed in large system development uses baseline versions which are made accessible to the project team. The team members then build test versions of parts of the system on top of these baseline versions. When these parts have been tested they are submitted for integration into the next base-line version of the system. This working procedure has many implications for the Ada program library and associated tools.

There are also problems arising from the need to create and maintain a significant number of baseline and test versions. Their solution places requirements on the linking mechanisms of the compilation system; for instance partial linking, also called incremental linking, can be beneficial in overcoming limitations of machine resources.

The high proportion of software reuse again affects the area of the Ada program library. Reusable software components can be considered products in their own right. Typically they are used by teams other than those who develop and maintain them. Therefore, they need to be imported into the Program Libraries where they are used.

The description of a program library in the Reference Manual is concerned only with the effects of compiling the units of a single program. In practice, especially in large system development, more powerful program library facilities are needed to support version and configuration management. Compilation systems vary widely in the program library facilities offered, and it is important to ensure that the facilities match the requirements.

In a large development, project items, such as source code, object code and documentation, may be kept in a database which is chosen for the purposes of project control and is unsuitable for direct use by the compilation system. In order to maintain the integrity of the project items the compilation system must provide some means to maintain the consistency of the program library with the database.

Examples of the requirements on the compilation system of large binary images are: address space limits, memory management aspects, segmentation aspects.

The large number of recompilations required may mean that different compilation systems must be used, one for development, when compilation time predominates, and another for production, when run-time efficiency is more important. Some facilities that can help are:

- automatic recompilation of all dependent units;

- reporting by the compilation system of recompilation or editing entailed by proposed changes;

- automatic avoidance by the compilation system of unnecessary recompilations, for example recompilation of units dependent on a package specification which has declarations added but none removed or altered;

- reduction of recompilation time by recompilation from an internal representation, so saving some reprocessing;

- incremental compilation, that is making use of the previous compiled version of a unit and processing only the changed parts.

4

Portability

It is frequently the case that there is a requirement to have the same application program running in more than one hardware or software environment. The requirement may stem from a variety of causes, but most are related to economics; others are related to consistency. Generally, if it is cheaper to rewrite a program for a different environment than to make it portable, then that is the way forward, and with this approach it is possible to take advantage of any beneficial characteristics of the new environment, or to add enhancements to the application. But sometimes it is important that the transported application should look and behave in exactly the same way as before, in which case transporting the existing program offers the best approach.

It is unlikely that the kind of application for which the Ada programming language was designed would be cheaply transported to a different environment by wholesale rewriting, and in fact Ada was designed with the intention that such rewriting would be unnecessary.

Portability, then, is a consideration which applies to non-trivial programs. Such programs are likely to involve significant investment in their development, and this investment needs to be preserved across changes in the environment. Minor environmental developments are a hazard which all program developers have to accommodate; ensuring that an application is proof against major changes in the environment requires special attention.

Whereas evolution of the environment may be the major portability concern of the application user, an application supplier may see the need to be able to distribute the final product to many users who, between them, use a variety of different environments. Portability then becomes a question of compatibility. Where the problem is one of an evolving environment, a degree of rewriting of the application may be acceptable, but where multiple environments have to be accommodated by the same product, special source code must be minimised if the application supplier is to avoid having to maintain very many variants of the same system.

4.1 Levels of Portability

There is no universally agreed definition of portability. Some take the view that portability involves no change at all to the source, just a recompilation and relinking. Others take the view that some change is inevitable, and in some cases may even be highly desirable, so as to take advantage of some characteristic of the new environment, for example. The latter view tends to be held by implementors of application programs which have a particularly low-level interface to their environments. A compilation system may go some way to addressing these particular requirements by providing standard interfaces for use between an application program and its environment. These interfaces typically encapsulate particular environment functions, and are supplied as part of the compilation system for each target environment. An approach to portability by an application program developer might be to devise such encapsulations where none exist in the compilation system chosen.

At the time of writing this Guide, binary compatibility across different environments is rare. Even when no rewriting of source code is required, it is usually necessary to recompile existing source before the application can run in a new environment. Even then, portability can only be achieved if there is a compatible compilation system for the new environment. Therefore the availability of compatible compilation systems for all actual and potential application environments should be considered when choosing any compilation system.

4.2   Problems with Portability

The question of compatibility of compilation systems is a complex one, even when bearing in mind that Ada is a standard language. The new environment may involve a different target computer on which the application program is to run, a different host computer on which the program is maintained, or both. There may be different operating systems on either computer. Although the Ada language is designed for the production of portable applications, there are many features which are under the control of the compiler developer and whose implementation may be influenced by the characteristics of the host and target computer systems. Compilation systems from different suppliers may implement these features in different ways. An application program developer must pay full attention to these characteristics and how these features are implemented in order to ensure that application programs are as portable as they need to be.

As yet there is no tool-set standard for the development and maintenance of programs in Ada, and therefore the tools used for program development are another factor to be taken into account when considering application portability. This can be a significant problem where maintenance procedures have been developed around a particular set of tools which have no direct counterpart in the new environment.

5

Compile-Time Operational Qualities

This chapter covers the operational qualities of the compilation system rather those of the application. Thus it is concerned with compile-time rather than run-time aspects. Broadly, these qualities are of interest to system developers whatever their application domain, although some characteristics of the application may colour their view of the tools in the system. Such characteristics include: the size of the system being developed; the ability of the development team; and whether the target is the same as or different from the host.

The following qualities may be considered:

- performance (speed and memory resource requirements);

- capacity (measure of the size and complexity of the program that can be compiled);

- reliability;

- robustness;

- scope (what facilities are provided);

- ease of use;

- integration (with other tools in the compilation system).

These qualities are discussed below. It is clear that they are not independent, and that different system developers assign them different priorities.

5.1   Performance

Generally, compile-time performance is less important for an end-user than run-time performance and therefore compile-time performance requirements are likely to be less visible at the start of an application development. However, unduly high consumption of host resources is not acceptable to the system developer. Generally slow performance of the compilation system may make interactive use of the tools impossible. Even if local custom and usage dictate a mainly batch mode, interactive use of the editor and debugger is usually preferred. Indeed the performance of the debugger may be crucial to its usability in developing some applications for instance those involving real-time processing.

5.2 Capacity

It is clearly important that the intended development machine should have enough storage capacity for the compilation system to be able to compile and link the application system. There are a number of ways in which the storage capacity can fall short, depending on the construction of the compilation system: the size of the compilation system itself, the size of unit that can be compiled, the total size of program that can be linked, and so on. Lack of sufficient capacity may make the compilation system unusable, or, at best, force the application developer into the difficult and time-consuming process of dividing the application into smaller parts.

5.3 Reliability

When developing anything it is necessary to have confidence in the tools that are being used. The reliability of the compilation system is paramount, especially when developing complex or safety-critical applications. In a mature compilation system it is probable that all but the most obscure errors have been found and corrected as the system matured. With the particularly complex tools in the compilation system errors may still be present as patterns of use can vary between system developers.

It is important when assessing the requirements for reliability to consider the types of possible errors. There are basically two types, those which make development more difficult, for example errors in the editor that can be seen immediately; and those which may result in inaccurate code being generated which is difficult to detect, for example errors in the compiler. The requirements for reliability of the application under development will influence the requirements for reliability of the compilation system.

It would be ideal to use a completely reliable compilation system, but at present complete reliability cannot be guaranteed by a supplier. At the time of writing this Guide there is in the market a probable trade off between reliability, complexity and cost. Also the practice of separately purchasing the tools within a compilation system without the benefit of a Public Tool Interface can lead to the reliability of the compilation system being less than that for the individual tools, due to interfacing difficulties.

5.4 Robustness

Whereas reliability is concerned with the behaviour of the compilation system when given valid input, robustness is the ability of the compilation system to cope with invalid input and other exceptional situations. One might reasonably expect that none of the tools in the compilation system would crash in such circumstances, but the recovery attempted and achieved may vary greatly between systems. While, for example, most compilation systems respond adequately to being presented with a syntactically incorrect program, in other cases the adequacy of the response varies greatly. For example a syntactically incorrect command may cause a tool to put the application system into an inconsistent state.

5.5 Scope

There is quite a wide range of features that each tool in the compilation system might possess. Tools, apart from the compiler, may be specific to Ada or they may be independent of the language. Some possibilities are outlined below.

5.5.1 Editor
The editor may be screen-oriented, line-oriented, or both. Line editors tend to be best suited to batch editing and screen editors to interactive editing. A further possibility is syntax-directed editors which are particularly useful for inexperienced users of the language.

5.5.2 Compiler
The Reference Manual contains a large number of implementation-dependent features. The absence of some of these, such as representation clauses, might make the compiler unusable for some applications. The validation summary report indicates which implementation-dependent features are supported. See chapter 31, Published Literature. As well as implementation-dependent features of the language, compilers may provide optional features in other ways, for instance by the use of parameters to the invocation commands.

5.5.3 Listing Tools
Tools that might be available include cross-referencers, formatters or pretty printers and tools to give listings in which fully expanded names appear explicitly. It may also be possible to obtain other information such as a representation of the structure of the program.

5.5.4 Linker
Linking should not provide opportunities for the rules of Ada to be contravened, for example, by allowing incompatible objects to be linked together accidentally. In some systems the linker itself prevents this happening, in others this is achieved by a different tool, for example a linker steering-file generator. The linker may be required to support additional facilities by some applications, for example distinguishing between ROM and RAM. A partial linking facility could be valuable when

testing parts of large systems or when parts of a large system become stable and therefore do not require continual relinking.

5.5.5 Target Loader

Target loading is the transfer of executable images from the host to the target. The various ways in which this can be carried out depends on the medium of transfer between the host and target. This medium could be a ROM, an intermediate medium such as a floppy disk or a communications link. The sophistication of the loader, and therefore the space it occupies on the target, if any, may vary depending on the requirements to handle complex target architectures. The physical form of the host-target link can affect performance of the target loader.

5.5.6 Debugger

A wide variety of features is possible in an Ada debugger, which can be used in a number of ways, for instance to identify errors in the application or as a testing tool for the application. Certain features, such as interacting with the user in Ada language terms to provide breakpoints, traces, reading and writing of variables and trapping of unhandled exceptions are considered important requirements. Full treatment of tasks and generics is also highly desirable. A comprehensive debugging language, for use in batch or interactive mode, can be valuable.

5.5.7 Library Manager

The Reference Manual defines a program library as containing the compilation units of a program, and mentions a library file which contains information concerning those units needed for separate compilation and linking. In practice a program library contains a consistent collection of compilation units, not necessarily constituting a single program and information about them.

The library manager provides, as a minimum, facilities for the creation, initialisation, and deletion of program libraries, and for maintaining libraries. The library maintenance function normally comprises: facilities to display the contents of a library, showing for each unit its compilation date, current state, and the units upon which it depends; facilities to mark a unit as invalid; and facilities to delete a unit.

The library manager is a point of interaction between the Ada compilation system and the development environment and its functions are not defined by the language. All the facilities the library manager provides are likely to be affected by the environment. This may result in incompatibilities between the Ada program library and the way that the system development uses the environment.

Some implementations may provide additional functionality, such as the ability to acquire units from other libraries, the ability to handle alternative or variant bodies of library units, or the ability to make more complex enquiries of the library manager. An example of this last functionality might be to enquire which other units must be recompiled if a particular unit is recompiled. An implementation may also go beyond the Reference Manual's concept of a single program library and support a hierarchical or other structure of connected but separate sub-libraries.

5.6 Ease of Use

Ease of use encompasses a number of aspects: the user interface; quality of error reports and integration of the tools in the compilation system.

The user interface to the compilation system may depend on the environment, for instance, it might use an available command line interpreter or a windowing system with icons, menus and similar facilities. The particular style chosen may depend on individual preferences, software development life cycle adopted and proficiency of the user. Some compilation systems might allow the style of the user interface to be chosen by the individual user.

In general, the quality of error reports is crucial. Ideally, the user should be able to select the form of message. This could vary from a terse form appropriate for experienced users to a verbose form for beginners.

5.7 Integration

An Ada compilation system comprises many component tools. The extent to which the individuality of the tools is apparent to the user is a measure of the integration that has been achieved in the system. However, a well designed user interface may give the illusion of a high degree of integration, even when integration is actually rather low. Therefore it is necessary to distinguish between tool integration and an integrated user interface.

To understand why tool integration may be important, it is necessary to consider what levels of integration might be possible. Since each tool may be integrated with the others to a different extent, it is appropriate to consider the levels as a continuum. At the low end, each component tool is a separate program. It takes its input from files and perhaps from the keyboard, performs whatever processing is necessary and leaves its results in files for use by other tools before terminating and allowing the next tool to be started. At the high end, the component tools interact through a common database, and share code where they perform some processing in common.

The kinds of advantages seen for high integration relate to integrity of the data and efficiency of operation. By maintaining data in a common database, there is less opportunity for the data to become corrupted through the operation of alien software. Where data is held in externally accessible files, there may be the temptation to patch a file to avoid having to recompile an incorrect source. Efficiency is improved if tools do not have to spend time opening files and checking the data before it is used, and more particularly, several components may be running simultaneously, passing data between each other as necessary. In such a system, it may be possible to detect errors much earlier than in a less well integrated system. An example of this might be that syntax errors can be detected and subprogram calling sequences checked as source code is entered.

There are also benefits to be had from low levels of tool integration, but these are of a different kind. Low levels of integration place much less severe demands on the hardware support required: the amount of code and data that needs to be on-line at any time may be much smaller than is required for high levels of integration. Typically, there will be more interfaces in the system, and if these are publicly defined, there is scope for introducing additional tools from third party suppliers, thus increasing the flexibility of the system. Such additional tools might provide facilities for analysing programs, or for providing interfaces to other languages or program development methods.

An integrated user interface may hide the underlying structure by allowing the user to set off a batch of individual tools as though they were a single tool. The way the batch is parameterised may leave the user completely unaware that several different tools are being activated, but the benefits of a high level of tool integration, particularly efficiency, will not be there. Nevertheless, integration at this level can add considerably to the ease with which it is possible to use a compilation system which has otherwise very little integration.

6

Software Interfacing

A program may exhibit the need for software interfacing at three points: between different components of the same program; with other programs in the same computing system, particularly with an operating system; and with other programs which may be in other processors or running at a different time.

6.1   Internal Interfaces

Detailed consideration of the use of Ada language features, such as procedure calls and parameter passing, for interfacing between components of an Ada program is outside the scope of this Guide. However, problems may arise when a system developer wishes to share program components between several programs, or to use pre-existing components. Such components might be made available as source, as compiled code, or in some intermediate or other format.

The use of compiled code obviates the need for compilation of a shared component for each program in which it is used, but restricts the scope of any global optimisation. Some other format may offer a compromise.

There are other factors which affect how shared or pre-existing components might best be made available. These include whether or not parameterisation from other components is required, and whether or not there is any impact from the target configuration. For example:

- the component may depend on declarations in another component which affect what compiled code sequences are optimal;

- the presence or absence of floating point hardware on the target may affect what code must be compiled for arithmetic operations;

- the amount of physical memory actually available may affect the choice of size for address fields and the use of segment addressing on the target.

Where the format of the component provides less flexibility than is needed, it might be useful for the system developer to maintain several variants of the same component and to select an appropriate variant depending on the context in which the component is to be used.

Whatever the format used for the distribution of commercially available Ada software libraries there are restrictions on the way in which the software may be incorporated. The choice of a compilation system may be dictated by the availability of software in the appropriate format for use with that compilation system.

For various reasons, usually concerned with protecting the supplier's investment, commercially available software is not generally distributed in source form but in a compiled format. Such software has to be incorporated directly into an Ada program library. Since there are, at the time of writing this Guide, no standards on the characteristics of an Ada program library, and what is even more significant, no standards for the run-time structure of a compiled Ada program, commercially available software distributed in this way may only be used in conjunction with program components compiled by the same compilation system. Even different versions of the same compilation system may lead to incompatibilities, and thus the supplier's policy and capability with regard to future releases of the compilation system are important considerations. Thus the mere existence of collections of commercially available software in program library format for use with a particular compilation system count for little, unless it can be established that it is the policy of the compilation system supplier to ensure that future releases of the compilation system remain compatible with the program library as it currently exists.

Commercially available software distributed in source form and compiled locally does not have these restrictions. However, other factors become relevant such as the size of each component in relation to the capacity of the compilation system, use of any language features not supported by the compilation system and any assumptions in the software about the characteristics of the target system.

Within an Ada program library the names of all components must be distinct identifiers. If, then, it is required to import two or more libraries into the same Ada program library, for example, a numerical library and a graphics library, it is necessary that the constituent components have been given distinct names or that some mechanism is provided for circumventing name clashes.

Apart from commercially available software written in Ada, there exists a wealth of software libraries in other languages. Many users may already have such software. The Ada pragma INTERFACE provides the mechanism whereby such software may be called from within an Ada program, but an Ada compilation system usually supports interfaces to only a limited set of other languages, unless a common calling convention has been established to which the Ada compilation system adheres.

Machine code is a specific case of another language and it may be written using the same interface conventions as compiled Ada code. However, a mechanism is still required to enable the introduction of a machine code component into an Ada program, whether through the Ada program library or otherwise.

An alternative means of interfacing to machine code is through the use of package MACHINE_CODE if it has been implemented in the compilation system. Such a facility has the potential to enable the system developer to implement interfaces to other software, but may be limited by the compilation system restrictions on the linking or building of programs containing foreign components.

The complementary facility whereby a piece of Ada code is called from code written in some other language requires the appropriate Ada run-time code environment to exist. It is conceivable that an integrated system might adopt a run-time code environment which is compatible across Ada and other selected languages, thus facilitating calls either way.

6.2 Operating System Interfaces

Although the Ada language was conceived for programming embedded computer systems where there is no separate operating system, not all applications for which Ada is suitable take this form. The facilities provided for interaction with any operating system are dependent on the implementation of the Ada compilation system. Typically, access is provided through one or more library units imported into or initialised as part of the Ada program library. Calls on these units may be treated specially, may possibly generate in-line code sequences, or may be handled by supplier-written code which makes the required operating system entries. Where library units are not supplied, it may be necessary for the system developer to write machine code sequences to make the necessary entries; this requires a compilation system that supports the use of machine code.

In general the operating system is invisible to the Ada program, although there is interaction when the operating system is invoked to perform some action or supply some information. Nevertheless an operating system, and perhaps the presence of other programs, might intrude upon the execution of a program in the following respects:

- absorption of processor time leading to fluctuations in elapsed execution time;

- varying availability of storage;

- varying restrictions on the maximum number of tasks;

- dynamic relocation of code and data in physical memory, which may be relevant if machine code has been used to record physical addresses.

A compilation system might provide facilities such as particular interfaces to the operating system to control the extent of these interactions.

6.3   Interfaces to Other Programs

If it is possible for one program to interface with another co-resident in the computer, it is usually achieved through calls to the operating system, although in some systems this operating system may be considered as an extension of the Ada run-time system. There is a general need for one program to interface with others which are not co-resident, and the primary concern here is for compatibility of data. Such interfaces consist of files, a special case being a communications channel.

There are many facets to this program-to-program interface which need to be examined since Ada does not define the physical format of a file. Even for a text file it is necessary to consider at least the character set, representation, maximum line length, line termination and file termination if it is to be used as an interface between two programs, particularly if one of the programs was not written in Ada. For other kinds of file it is necessary to consider the representation of basic and user defined types, array and record packing, the presence of any control fields and the overall file structure.

Factors which may affect whether or not two Ada programs can interface using the same file are:

- whether or not the programs share all relevant type declarations;

- whether or not the programs were compiled with the same version of the compilation system;

- whether or not the programs were compiled with the same compilation system;

- whether or not the programs are executed under the control of the same operating system.

Where compatibility cannot be guaranteed across the file interface, it may be possible to use a combination of Ada representation specifications and the generic function UNCHECKED_CONVERSION to construct or interpret an alien file.

7

Run-Time Operational Qualities

The qualities of the run-time facilities and behaviour of an Ada program are of interest to most application developers, but for some they are of vital importance. The presence or absence of some features and the efficiency of the compilation system may permit or preclude some desirable strategy for the implementation of a given application or may indeed determine whether Ada can be used at all.

The purpose of this chapter is to examine the qualities which characterise the run-time facilities. The set of such qualities includes:

- performance, that is the size and execution speed of generated code and of the run-time system;

- predictability of program performance;

- efficiency of run-time storage management;

- how tasking is controlled on multi-processor systems;

- the strategy for exception handling;

- fairness of scheduling;

- how a program interacts with the environment and other programs;

- robustness of both generated code and the run-time system.

These qualities are considered below, from the viewpoint of the application system developer. Although each is considered separately there are areas of interaction and these are noted.

7.1 Performance

For many applications performance is a vital consideration, affecting either the capability of the application system or the total resources, including cost, which must be used to achieve a specified level of capability. Indeed for some critical applications too low a performance level may eliminate a particular compilation system from consideration. For the purposes of this section performance includes storage requirements as well as code execution speed.

The overall level of performance of an application is dependent on a number of different factors. Some, such as the chosen hardware configuration and the design and implementation of the application itself, are not the concern of this chapter, which is restricted to consideration of the generated code and the run-time system support code.

The effect of the code generated by the compilation system on application system performance is both direct and obvious. If the compiler generates code which is inefficient then the application executes slowly, and if the generated code occupies excessive space there may be problems in fitting the application into the target machine. These characteristics are under the control of the compilation system developer.

The effect that the run-time system has on performance is also extremely important but it is not so obvious; first, it has an effect through the storage space occupied by its code and data, and second, it has an effect through the time it takes to perform services on behalf of the application code.

Many real-time applications are required to manage the interactions between different parts of a program which must execute in parallel. Through its tasking facilities, Ada provides structures and mechanisms which are designed to simplify the coding of such programs. However, while these facilities may prove to be well-suited to the construction of a logically correct program, the performance of the tasking mechanisms may not be high enough to achieve adequate performance for the application.

7.2   Predictability of Programme Performance

Where there are no real-time issues, then the average performance of a system may be all that needs to be considered. However, if response time is an important factor, it is necessary to consider performance more closely.

One way to determine whether or not a system can meet the required response times is to consider its worst-case performance. However, if the performance of the application is likely to vary widely under different conditions, this approach can lead to the acquisition of a computer system which, for most purposes, is grossly overpowered and uneconomic. Therefore, the usual approach is to carry out a detailed analysis of the processing involved at all the points in the application where response time is critical. Such an analysis requires knowledge, not only of the application, but also of the performance of the individual components of the run-time support software.

The behaviour of the run-time support software is not necessarily predictable, being derived from a complex interaction of system components. In consequence, there may be variations in performance between executions of the same functions. Some of the major contributors to this variability can be storage management, interrupts, backing store accesses, scheduling variability, and the lengths of various queues and tables. This problem is aggravated by any other programs running in the same machine. A high quality design for a run-time system identifies what scope there is for variations in performance, and incorporates features which maintain these variations within controlled limits. The supplier of the compilation system should describe how an application may benefit from these features. In this way it is possible both to identify the spread of performance, function by function, and also to plan the application program to avoid creating the conditions under which performance is less predictable.

7.3 Efficiency of Run-Time Storage Management

The run-time system is responsible for the management of run-time storage in the application and some consideration must be given to the effects of this on the application. A number of different aspects are relevant and of particular relevance are storage for tasks and handling of dynamically allocated variables.

There are many options for the management of task storage open to the implementor of a compilation system. These yield trade offs between the number of tasks which can be created, the maximum amount of storage for each task and the overheads of task switching, creation and deletion.

The main concern for storage of dynamically allocated variables lies not in its allocation but in its recovery. Some run-time systems recover storage only when the corresponding declaration is out of scope. In this case if the application must run for a long period then special steps may need to be taken to avoid running out of store. This may include the use of deallocation procedures if they are provided.

If, however, the run-time system supports automatic recovery of storage for dynamically allocated variables then this probably involves a garbage collector. The use of a garbage collector may result in the execution of the application program being suspended at arbitrary times. This leads to unpredictable behaviour which is likely to be unacceptable for real-time applications.

7.4 Control of task allocation

On multi-processor systems the run-time system may support true parallel task execution. In this case the run-time system may provide facilities to control the allocation of tasks to processors. An example of such a facility is the ability to lock tasks on to particular processors.

7.5 Strategy for Exception Handling

Ada provides facilities for trapping exceptional conditions at run-time and passing control to handler routines supplied as part of the application program. In generating code to deal with exceptions a compiler may be optimised for either minimum overhead in normal operation or fastest handling of exceptions when raised, or may offer this choice to the user. The strategy adopted may be of special importance to time-critical applications. An example of an application needing fast handling of exceptions is a safety monitoring system, normally lightly loaded but needing a quick response to its own failure.

It is also important for the application developer to be aware of how the run-time system deals with exceptions for which there is no handler. Although if an unhandled exception occurs, Ada requires that the current task or main program be terminated, the run-time system may support diagnostic facilities to determine the cause of the exception.

7.6 Fairness of Scheduling

It is usual for applications to require the run-time system to support a fair system of scheduling tasks in an Ada program. When there are several ready tasks of equal priority, selection of one to run should not favour any task or group of tasks at the expense of others.

Whilst the Reference Manual describes the operation of the scheduling process in respect of tasks with different priorities, the order of scheduling is not defined. Although a scheduler which repeatedly schedules one group of tasks for execution to the exclusion of another group may conform to the language definition, it would probably not be a suitable base for building a real-time system.

When there is a possible choice of tasks to rendezvous with a particular task, the order of selection is not defined by the language, but for many applications it is important that the selection process be fair.

7.7 Interactions with environment and other software

It is not a very useful program that does not interact with its environment in some way. Interaction may be explicit, calls on system functions and the exchange of messages, or implicit, consumption of resources such as storage and processor cycles. The Ada language provides a number of mechanisms for explicit interaction with the environment, the most obvious being the input-output packages. These packages provide for the use of sequential or direct access files, text oriented devices, and also for the basic control at the primitive device level. The nature of the environment may be such that it is not sensible for the run-time system to provide support to all these facilities. For example, where programs are to run under the control of an operating system, accesses to the control registers of peripheral devices may be strictly inhibited, whereas if the target is an embedded microprocessor, there may be no value in supporting a filing system. Neither of these is necessarily so: the operating system may support the addition of special device drivers; the embedded target may have extensive backing storage, perhaps as a RAM disc. The needs of the application must be clearly identified to avoid the risk of selection of a compilation system with inappropriate input-output support.

Another mechanism by which a program may interact with its environment is the interrupt, and this is supported by the Ada language. Again this support is usually more pertinent to embedded microprocessors, but can also be required to handle responses to asynchronous signals from an operating system or perhaps another program.

The Ada language does not explicitly provide support for a program to interact with an operating system or with other programs, but mechanisms exist which can be used to serve this purpose. The application developer may be able to write support code, not necessarily entirely in Ada, which enables application programs to use these mechanisms to communicate. Alternatively, the equivalent facilities may be provided as part of the run-time system supplied. Typically the mechanism used is a package of subprograms which enable parameters to be passed to or through the operating system. Where an application requires programs to interact, it is necessary to analyse precisely what forms of interaction are required, the quantities of data involved and the throughput, as different run-time system approaches may result in markedly different capabilities.

7.8 Robustness

It is important that at run-time a program should be robust, in the sense that its execution should not be interrupted, terminated, or otherwise adversely affected by incorrect code generated by the compiler, incorrect linking of the code, or by errors in the run-time system. If any such errors are known to exist they must be fully documented so that the developer can avoid them or mitigate their effects.

Robustness of programs in the sense of predictable and useful behaviour in the face of errors or unexpected events at the application level is a matter for the application developer and is not directly considered here. Note however that a run-time system may provide facilities to support the development of robust applications, such as an interface to initiate consistency checking.

8

Concurrency

This chapter is concerned with concurrency in the real world. This characterises an application in which a number of activities may be progressing at more or less the same time. The interaction between these parallel activities may be slight or there may be tight coupling requiring a high degree of synchronisation. A classic example of a system which must handle real-world concurrency is air traffic control. Each aircraft in the controlled airspace represents a separate activity which, of itself, has minimal interaction with the activities corresponding to other aircraft but which nevertheless makes competitive demands on the environment. The control system is responsible for introducing order among these concurrent activities.

Concurrency in the real world does not necessarily require concurrency in any related computer system. Often, in practice, it may be acceptable for the computer system to serialise its management of the real-world activities or to impose some other form of scheduling based on priority, which essentially has the effect of serialisation. However, serialisation on its own is not enough: except in the simplest of systems, concurrent activities typically compete for the same resources, and the computer system's scheduling algorithm must take account of this.

Where a computer system has advance information on the resource requirement profile over time of the activities it is managing, it can organise its scheduling appropriately. Where it does not have this information, it may need to have the capability of recovering from circumstances where two or more activities are mutually blocking one another's progress. This problem in concurrency is sometimes known as a "deadly embrace" and occurs in its simplest form when each of two concurrent activities holds a resource which the other needs before it can continue. Avoidance of a deadly embrace may require serialisation even in a multiprocessor system.

In the air traffic control example, the resources for which there is competition are the air space and runways. At the present stage of development, it is the human air traffic controller who is largely responsible for scheduling the use of these resources whilst the computer system tracks each aircraft concurrently and warns of potential conflicts. One of the resources that may need to be considered when scheduling concurrent activities is time. In terms of time, there are basically two kinds of activity: those that can wait or can be made to wait, and those which progress inevitably. Serialisation may suit the former, but for the latter some form of pre-emptive scheduling or parallel processing in the computer system is likely to be a necessity, with priorities assigned to events rather than activities.

A computer system may have to allocate time as a resource to concurrent activities in different ways. For example, a multi-user interactive system may need to be event driven as far as key strokes are concerned, to echo the key strokes to the user's terminal within the reaction time expected by the user, but may serialise the operations resulting from fully typed commands where the user can tolerate a less than immediate response.

A factor which is also dependent on the kind of activities involved is the determination of computing resources required. Where an activity can wait, inadequate computing resources will slow things down; if an activity cannot wait, inadequate computing resources leads to a failure of the system. Such a failure may be, for example, that the system overlooks a significant event.

Apart from computing resources required to support the average work load, additional resources may be needed to accommodate peak loads. It is not necessarily the case that the requirements for resources are linearly related to the work load. High levels of loading may give rise to disproportionately increased overheads in the computer system. It may even be necessary to set limits on the number of concurrent activities that can be managed at any one time to maintain the overheads in the system within acceptable levels. Overheads may result from combinatorial scheduling choices and the management of large numbers of system objects.

Serialisation of concurrency is implicit in a single processor system. A multiprocessor system may reflect some of the real-world concurrency in the computer system, although in general, it is not the practice to provide a processor for each activity unless these activities are fixed in number and have stringent requirements for computing power. Perhaps a rather special case of the latter is an array processor which provides the means for each element of a vector or array to be operated upon in parallel.

Interaction between concurrent activities is another application aspect which varies widely. In the traffic control system cited above, one of the objectives is to eliminate direct interaction; in an array processing application, there must be frequent synchronisation points.

The fundamental requirements for systems to support real-world concurrency, then, are to have enough computing power and other resources available at the right time. In some cases it may be acceptable to delay things so that computing resources can be provided as available, whereas in others, events must be handled in accordance with deadlines of varying severity.

The Ada language was designed with concurrency in mind, and provides the means, where appropriate, for the application developer to assign a thread of control corresponding to each real-world parallel process. Each thread of control is represented by an Ada task, and tasks may be fixed in number or created dynamically, depending on the needs of the application.

Concurrency

In order to exchange data, tasks may rendezvous with one another, or they may access common areas of data. Inevitably there are overheads in the services a compilation system provides for the management of multiple tasks. These overheads are apparent in the work that needs to be carried out by the run-time system to schedule tasks, to create new tasks dynamically, and handle the inter-task communication. The behaviour of the task scheduler, particularly with regard to its treatment of priorities and any attempt it might make to ensure that the resources of the processor are fairly distributed among the tasks, can influence the performance of the resulting application system. Target hardware is often designed with an architecture intended to ensure that the processing of parallel tasks can be performed efficiently. The extent to which the Ada run-time system takes advantage of any such features can also have a marked effect on performance.

9

Security

Security concerns the protection of information from unauthorised access. It may be divided into the preservation of secrecy, that is the prevention of unauthorised reading, and the preservation of integrity, that is the prevention of unauthorised writing. In general the requirements for maintaining secrecy and integrity are similar.

Mechanisms for control of access to information are of two kinds. In discretionary access control, the power to permit or deny access to any information is at the discretion of the owner of that information. In mandatory access control, rules based on the security classification of information and the clearance of the user are enforced by the system.

Requirements on the compilation system can arise from the security aspects of both the application to be developed and the development process itself, though these are often connected.

9.1 Security Aspects of the Application

Examples of security aspects of the application to be developed are verification, dataflow, and security of the run-time system.

There may be a requirement to verify, more or less formally, the code against its specification, particularly with regard to the security model. Present verification techniques work only if certain features of the Ada language are avoided, as for instance in the SPARK subset (Carré and Jennings 1988). It is convenient if the compilation system offers a means of enforcing such restrictions. It is also possible that the compilation system offers support for formal verification.

A principle of mandatory access control is that information must not flow from a higher level of security to a lower. The application developer must decide to what units the security levels are to apply, for example task, package, compilation unit, or program. This decision must take into account the facilities offered by the compilation system. Assistance by the compilation system in analysing dataflow across security levels is then highly desirable.

If there is a run-time system to be incorporated in the final system, then it must be subjected to as careful security analysis as the rest of the channels, for instance for covert channels. A covert channel is any means by which information may be passed in a way that circumvents the security system.

9.2 Security of the Development Process

Security requirements on the development process may arise from the requirements of the system under development, for example because implementation details of a highly secure system need to be restricted. Examples of relevant considerations are access control, and the security rating of the compilation system.

Access control and monitoring must be considered for source, object code, listings, journals, and all internal forms: symbol tables, intermediate code. It should be remembered that the source can be, partly or wholly, reconstructed from some internal representations for example Diana.

It is possible that the security rating of the compilation system plus its host operating system can be ascertained from widely accepted evaluation criteria (DoD Computer Security Center 1983). Otherwise it may be necessary to undertake a security analysis.

An example of an integrity requirement on the development and maintenance system imposed by the security requirements of the application system is the need to prevent unauthorised tampering with the object code of the application system, for example by patching. This is needed to prevent the introduction of code to breach the application system's secrecy controls (Trojan horses) or its integrity controls (worms and viruses).

10

Timing Constraints

Response times are critical requirements for some applications. An application system may be required to take timely action in response to user commands or external stimuli. The importance of meeting these requirements varies according to the application, but is most severe in those applications where data is only available for short periods before it is lost, or else must be sampled regularly so that changes in value can be related to specific periods. Examples of such applications include radar systems where the relationships between the echo data and the direction of the scanner must be strictly maintained.

There are a number of ways the timing constraints of the application system can be expressed. The requirements on the performance may be stated in statistical terms, for example as an average throughput of messages, or in absolute terms, for example that a response must be given to an event within a stated number of seconds. Frequently both maximum response time and average throughput are given in terms of some statistical distribution in time of the assumed occurrence of the events. There may also be requirements on the acceptable level of input data missed when the application system is unable to maintain control of data capture as well as producing the response.

A prime requirement on any compilation system to be used in the production of an application system with timing constraints is that the generated code and the Ada run-time system are sufficiently efficient.

Almost as important as the speed of response is the predictability of the Ada program's response time. That is, the same path through the code should take approximately the same time each time it is executed except for higher priority interrupts. In critical cases enough information should be provided by the compilation system supplier about the run-time performance to confirm the required upper bounds on the path execution times. An often quoted example which contravenes this requirement is an automatic garbage collector which suspends the program's normal operation unpredictably. This is unacceptable in application systems with stringent timing constraints.

Another possible requirement is long-term stability of performance. For an application system which is expected to run for hours, days or weeks without restarting, it is necessary that its performance should not be progressively degraded. Degradation might occur as a consequence of a loss of available storage due to fragmentation or unrecovered storage for dynamically allocated variables. This is a case when an automatic garbage collector can be valuable.

Many of these requirements can be met by appropriate design of the application program. Comprehensive documentation of the characteristics and limitations of the tasking and storage management systems help the application developer to achieve an appropriate design. For example, if an automatic garbage collector is used, the application developer needs to be aware of this. Facilities are required to invoke a garbage collector in a controlled way or information is required from the compilation system supplier as to how to avoid needing to invoke the garbage collector.

An application system which responds to randomly occurring stimuli, or where the processing requirements associated with a stimulus vary widely, has the potential to succumb to a condition known as overload. Overload is progressive and occurs typically when there is insufficient time to complete the processing for one stimulus before further data requiring processing arrives. Although, depending on the severity of the timing constraints, it is usually possible to accommodate short peaks, a continuing high data rate eventually leads to data being lost. Any ability an application system has to protect itself from overload is important. Load shedding can be achieved by assigning low priorities to the tasks which perform background activity and high priority to those tasks which perform time-critical processing. With a compilation system which implements priority scheduling, the low priority tasks are then not scheduled until there is time available. It is possible for an Ada run-time system to go further than this and to make available to an application program information about missed interrupts or scheduler activity, for example through calls to supplied subprograms. How this information is made available and how it may be used is likely to be a selling feature of any compilation system designed for time-critical applications.

Another useful feature is a performance prediction facility which generates a graph showing the paths of control through the program and which annotates each arc of the program graph with an indication of how long it takes to execute that path. It is also useful to have an indication by the compilation system where a usually expensive Ada construct is employed.

The monitoring and testing of systems with timing constraints, especially if they are very stringent, also needs consideration. There may well not be sufficient spare performance in the target computer system to allow for software for monitoring and testing. Therefore there is a need for other options to monitor and test the application system, for example logic analysers and in-circuit emulators, and the compilation system must support their use. These facilities are especially necessary during acceptance testing of the performance of the application system as measured by response time and data missed.

Ada defines a number of features which provide for high level or detailed interaction with the application environment, many of which are particularly

Timing Constraints

relevant to time-critical application systems. At the time of writing this Guide, implementation of all these features is not always enforced. Typically time-critical application systems need to be able to respond to hardware interrupts and to perform operations at the level of input-output drivers. It may be necessary to write some instructions in machine code to be able to call routines written in some other language, usually a low-level language such as assembly code or the programming language C. If parallel tasks are required, then so is a well implemented priority scheduling system, but for some time-critical applications, particularly those that are designed to work synchronously, Ada tasking may be inappropriate. The run-time system should be such as to ensure that the application system can make full use of the accuracy and precision of whatever real-time clock is installed in the target hardware. The application system should be able to use the predefined input-output packages or their equivalent without impeding the running of its time-critical tasks.

11

Host-Target Development

Host-target development is the term used here to describe the method of application system development in which the eventual target computer for the application system is used in conjunction with the computer on which most of the development is carried out, called the host. The term is used even if the target used during development differs in some respects from the eventual target, the essential feature being that the host provides additional computing resources to support the development process. Often the host and target are physically linked at some stage, but this is not essential. In some cases the host may be the same type of computer or even the same physical computer as the target, but with a different environment.

Reasons for using a host-target development system vary. Often there is no suitable development system on the target computer, perhaps because it lacks the necessary resources or is too specialised. Again, the development may be too large to use the target system, even though it could support a smaller project. It may be that the application developer's policy is to use a particular host, for example to accommodate a number of different targets, to exploit a set of tools that has been built up, or to exploit accumulated experience in the use of the host.

The host-target development method has its own problems and requirements on the compilation system. The time taken to transfer a program from the host to the target is often a bottleneck in the development cycle. Efficient crossloading and downloading techniques are essential. Even so, it is usually desirable to do as much testing and debugging on the host as possible. This may present problems if the compilation systems for the host and target are different, particularly if they are from different suppliers, as implementation-defined features are likely to differ significantly.

It is always necessary to do some testing on the target, and facilities for controlling this from the host are desirable, for instance interactive debugging from the host of a program running on the target. For some application developments, support of hardware debugging aids such as in-circuit emulators and programmable logic analysers may be required.

12

Embedded Application Systems

The term "embedded" is usually applied to an application system which is a component of some larger system, for example radar equipment. However it does not serve the purposes of this Guide to produce a rigid definition for the term; it is more useful to identify the particular characteristics which may be found in embedded application systems and which are generally of lesser significance in others.

As a component, the application system is not generally able to communicate directly with a human operator. It responds to and manipulates other items of equipment which may possibly themselves have a human interface. It is also possible that no human interaction is involved at all. Thus for many such systems, textual manipulation is of limited importance and is not always supported by compilation systems where the target is expected to be an embedded processor.

An embedded application system does not generally require the support of a conventional data processing file system. Where large quantities of stored data are involved, these are either held in large arrays in main memory or in dedicated files, that is, files which are always associated with the programs. Some kind of log file or channel may however be required for monitoring the application. Again, compilation systems for embedded application systems often do not provide the predefined packages associated with bulk file storage.

Typically, much of the input and output of an embedded application system is not file oriented in the conventional sense at all. In many cases, it may not even be byte or word oriented. Control and sensing of individual bits at specific hardware addresses over highways of various widths are required. Thus a compilation system is required which allows the embedded application system to respond to hardware interrupts and to perform operations at the level of input-output drivers. It may be necessary for the application system implementor to write some instructions in machine code or to be able to call routines written in some other language, usually a low-level language such as assembly code or the programming language C.

Precise control and measurement of timing are also often essential. One aspect of timing is that the program for an embedded application system may be expected to function at rates within prescribed bounds. That is, it may be essential for the program to perform some function within a specified time for some event, or else its deviation from some response time must be predictable or controlled. This implies that the run-time system should be such as to ensure that the application system can make full use of the accuracy and provision of whatever real-time clock is installed in the target hardware.

Resilience is a very important factor where human intervention is undesirable or impossible. An embedded system may be expected to accommodate both external and internal perturbations and catastrophes. The required response of the embedded application may be full recovery, continued operation but with reduced capability, or execution of some final limited functions in the case of a catastrophe. Values out of range is an example of an external perturbation; failure of consistency checks is an example of an internal perturbation. More serious may be the failure of some component of the larger system itself. Resilience involves the handling of unexpected events, not just problems that have been anticipated. Continued operation may depend on a prompt response just once in a lifetime of operation, and it may be acceptable to incur considerable overheads in normal operation to ensure this. Alternatively, such resilience as is needed may be provided by other subsystems of the larger system, and therefore any overheads automatically introduced by the compilation system to provide it may be an unacceptable burden.

The performances required of embedded application systems cover a wide range from idling to heavily computational. Programs may be single-threaded or may involve a degree of parallelism. Where parallelism is involved, this may require rapid or relatively infrequent switching between activities. Switching may be required on the basis of interrupts, priorities, time slices or work content. Multiple processors may operate with various degrees of coupling, with or without shared storage. Each different compilation system has its own strategy for handling and scheduling parallel tasks, and it is unlikely that any provides optimum facilities for all application techniques. Therefore it is important to understand what are the requirements an application has with regard to scheduling, and to check whether or not potential compilation systems address these requirements.

There is wide variation in the architectures of the different processors used for embedded application systems, often manifested in the addressing ranges available and the addressing techniques used. There may be hardware or system constraints which dictate how the address space is used: which ranges are available for RAM, which for ROM and which for special purposes; which for code and which for data; how much storage can be linearly addressed at any one time; how storage is segmented; how overheads may arise for different kinds of references. Different kinds of applications may make different, special demands on this architecture.

Embedded application systems generally store the code in ROM. Where there is a quantity of constant data, it is desirable that this be in ROM also. In some application systems, it is required that code or data can be changed by the replacement of plug-in modules. Thus a compilation system is likely to be required that provides a high degree of control over the placement of code and data. Although Ada provides facilities for defining the locations of entities in the source code, use of this feature limits the flexibility available to the application system developer, and control at, for example, the program linker, or even the target loader level may be more useful. This is particularly true with modern target architectures where there is considerable flexibility for mapping between physical and logical address spaces.

In common with other components of the larger system, an embedded application system is usually replicated many times. Thus there is pressure to keep the hardware component count low, simply for economic reasons. The nature of the application can also dictate low weight and size, and consequently compactness and efficiency are required from the output of the compilation system. This in turn dictates that compiled code and data should be compact.

Although an embedded application system can be tested at various stages of its development, as completion of the development nears, the testing process becomes more difficult. The need is to provide the application system with a sufficiently realistic environment but to introduce minimal degradation of its performance as a result of any test aids. Since there are frequently aspects of operation which cannot be given a live test, some means of predicting the larger system's behaviour may be necessary. This might be provided in the compilation system, either by adequate documentary descriptions of the code that would be compiled under a wide variety of circumstances, together with statements of performance, or by tools for analysing and predicting performance of compiled code under a variety of conditions.

13

Hardware Interfacing

By "hardware interfacing" is meant the means by which the installed software responds to and affects its environment. The environment is to be considered as external to or local to the application computer system as appropriate.

Depending on the nature of the application computer system, certain hardware interfacing may be assumed to be supplied as standard. For example, in many computer systems, the interfaces to a user terminal and to backing storage devices have this characteristic. In more primitive computer systems, such interfaces must be programmed explicitly, as must interfaces to non-standard devices, that is devices not directly supported by the supplier of the processor. Similarly, for paged or segmented main storage, it is generally assumed that compiled code automatically contains instructions to manipulate address registers and paging tables as necessary to ensure correct execution of the program. However, for an application which is of the nature of systems software, the application developer may need to manipulate these directly.

There are two principal programming mechanisms by which processors exchange data with external hardware. One mechanism makes use of special-purpose instructions, effectively identifying an input-output address space. The other mechanism uses regular data manipulation instructions operating on reserved addresses in the same address space as internal data (memory-mapped input-output). Additionally a hardware interrupt method may be available to allow a device to signal the processor. A limited amount of information is conveyed by virtue of the forced change in the processor's execution address caused by the interrupt.

The Ada language offers several mechanisms which may be implemented in a compilation system to enable an application developer to use special input-output instructions or memory-mapped input-output. The primary facility for this purpose is a package of target-dependent subprograms providing low-level access to the registers associated with peripheral devices. The compilation system may also allow the application developer to include machine code statements in an Ada program, thus giving direct use of input-output instructions. The Ada language itself has facilities which enable an application developer to associate particular variables with any memory-mapped input-output addresses, but at the time of writing this Guide, there is no guarantee that any particular compilation system implements this feature. Where implemented, the feature may also allow the application developer to arrange for particular tasks to be scheduled in response to interrupts from peripheral devices. A further facility of the language which is not always implemented enables an Ada program to make calls on subprograms which have been written in some other language, such as assembly code, and which could be used to address hardware directly.

Access to address registers, page and segmentation tables and other architectural features is often provided by the compilation system in a way similar to that in which access to input-output control is provided. However, it is often the case that hardware having a paged or segmented architecture protects its addressing control mechanisms through the use of privilege levels whereby application programs run at a level which does not permit access to these mechanisms; the mechanisms are available only to program code running at a sufficiently privileged level. Program control may be transferred from a less to a more privileged level usually by means of a special trap instruction, sometimes known as a software interrupt. A software interrupt may have many of the characteristics of a hardware interrupt and the same Ada facilities might be applied. Software interrupts might also be generated through attempts to use a privileged instruction at an insufficiently privileged level, but such an action could be expected to result in an exception being raised.

14

Exploitation of Target and Computational Capacity

Tradition has it that the only way to exploit fully the capabilities of computer hardware is to program in assembly code, or at least in some language which provides complete access to all the machine instructions and facilities. High-level languages are often viewed as a barrier between the programmer and the effective demonstration of his art. Ada was conceived for use in embedded application systems where the full potential of the hardware is required to be realised, however different compilation systems provide varying degrees of exploitation of the hardware.

Different applications demand efficiency in different areas, and target hardware architectures require exploitation in different ways to deliver that efficiency. Thus optimal benefits result from well considered matching between the hardware, the compilation system and the application.

A fundamental question of efficiency concerns the use of types and sizes of storage units used for arithmetic. If the hardware has been chosen for its support of arithmetic of the kinds predominating in the application, then it would be reasonable to apply the same criteria to selection of the compilation system. For example, if the hardware has been selected for its ability to perform integer arithmetic on bytes, then the compilation system would be expected to support variables of this size and to make use of the corresponding arithmetic instructions. Similar considerations apply to larger integers and the real numbers required by the application.

Often, floating point operations are provided through hardware which also provides additional numerical functions such as sine and cosine. Although Ada does not offer these as part of the language, it is open to a supplier of a compilation system to make such functions available through, for example, a library package. At the time of writing this Guide, a proposed standard for an elementary functions package seems likely to be adopted by ISO in the near future. How such a package is integrated with the compilation system affects the efficiency of use of the hardware functions. Where the hardware interface does not map well to the Ada language, facilities might be provided for accessing such functions through machine code statements or some other mechanism.

Hardware manufacturers devise a variety of architectures for targets which typically offer a wide range of configuration options to the application developer. This enables the application developer to tailor the target more closely to the application. By, for example, choosing the amount and type of storage to be used, mixing storage modules of different speeds if that is appropriate. The compilation system should take account of this flexibility in the mechanisms used for deciding where different classes of data and code are to be located.

Sometimes a target architecture introduces constraints of which the application developer might prefer to be unaware, such as the size of a page of code or data. A compilation system might force such constraints to the application developer's attention, or it might hide them with varying degrees of effectiveness.

It is often the case that, over the range of a family of targets, differences of detail, special features and developments combine so that program operations are achieved optimally in different ways. The compilation system may be able to cope with these differences by generating different machine-code sequences for the same Ada statements from its knowledge of the target machine, for example knowledge of whether the target has a floating point processor. However if different source code is required, the application developer might benefit from a means of directing the compilation system to compile just one from a set of alternative source code sequences. Where there is source code compatibility, some form of link-time or run-time discrimination might be appropriate, thus enabling the same program to be executed on a range of targets without recompilation.

The frequency of the system clock is another feature which may vary across a family of targets and this should be reflected accurately in the compilation system implementation of the Ada language timing features.

In addition to the special arithmetic functions which may be provided by hardware, modern targets are often designed with multitasking in mind, and consequently often provide special instructions intended for rapid task switching and environment control. How these special instructions are utilised by the compilation system and their value to an Ada program is pertinent to the selection of both the hardware and the compilation system.

Other machine-code instructions may be available to assist with, for example, range checks, fixed point operations, scheduling, stack handling, subprogram calls and parameter passing. If the compilation system does use these directly they might still be available to the application developer through the use of machine-code statements or interfaces to assembly code modules where these facilities are supported by the compilation system.

It is important to be aware that full use of the target instruction set does not necessarily guarantee the best implementation of the application. It is generally advisable to consider selection of hardware and the compilation system together.

15

Multiprocessing

The use of multiple processors, processing elements or complete computers in a computer system results from the need to meet objectives of a variety of kinds. Factors which affect whether multiprocessing is appropriate for an application include:

- processing power: a single processor may not be powerful enough;

- economics: the requirements may be met more economically through the use of several smaller processors than through the use of a single larger processor;

- flexibility: the number of processors can be chosen to match the size of the computing task;

- redundancy: processors are, to a limited extent, expendable, failures leading to progressive system degradation rather than immediate collapse;

- standby facility: a change over to an alternative processor can be achieved swiftly;

- specialisation: processors may be optimised for specific tasks;

- distribution: processing power may be applied at the places it is required;

- security: security barriers may be more easily policed between separate machines than within a single machine;

- simplicity: the system may be more easily engineered or managed across a collection of processors than within a single processor.

Consideration of these factors does not automatically lead to the use of multiple processors as the optimum solution for every application.
As implied above, a processor in this context may be anything from the most basic computing element to a complete computer. In particular, main storage may be shared or partially shared by multiple processors, or alternatively the only means of communication between processors may be

through backing store or message channels. The terms "loosely coupled" and "tightly coupled" are often used to classify multiprocessor systems, although the division in the classification is by no means clear cut.

15.1 Loosely Coupled Systems

A loosely coupled system is one in which the individual processors are relatively self-contained elements, usually running their own programs. Little if any main storage is shared; where main storage is shared it is likely to be for common program code in ROM, or perhaps an area of RAM used for message passing between processors. More usually, processors communicate by messages passed through channels, where a channel may be, for instance, a bus or a local area network. If main storage is not shared, it is possible for different processors to use different word lengths, even different data formats, with appropriate conversions taking place as part of the message interchange protocol. In particular, the separate processors may be of different manufacture having software with distinct origins. Thus there is the compatibility of the software to be considered. A loosely coupled system may also imply loosely coupled software, that is, the software used on one processor may not depend very strongly on the software used on another processor.

A loosely coupled system is appropriate where separate programs can be run on the individual processors and there is a relatively low level of interaction between programs, as may be the case with a distributed system. Since the channels of communication between different parts of the system are well defined, usually physically, it is a structure which can simplify the policing of security within the system.

In systems which are required to be highly reliable, it is essential that the failure of a processor has minimal impact on the operation of the system. A suitably structured loosely coupled system may allow a processor to be manually or automatically removed from the system and replaced, or to have its local storage modified, without the need to stop the system as a whole.

15.2 Tightly Coupled Systems

A collection of processors may be considered to be tightly coupled for any of several reasons, for example:

- The processors may share all or a major part of their main storage.

- They may all execute the same set of programs in some kind of load sharing arrangement.

Multiprocessing

- They may be so tightly coupled that they all execute the same instructions in synchronism.

This last case illustrates the functioning of the single instruction multiple data (SIMD) kind of array processor. For many purposes, such an array processor may be regarded much like a single processor with a single instruction stream, albeit with arrays rather than elements as data units, and having some special array operations. The multiple instruction multiple data (MIMD) kind of array processor involves a greater awareness of parallelism in its programming, with the coupling being through synchronisation points rather than instruction synchronism.

Yet another form of very tight coupling occurs with pipelining systems (not to be confused with processing units whose internal operations are pipelined) wherein data is passed along the line of processors, each of which performs some specific action as part of the overall operation of the program.

One of the distinguishing features of a tightly coupled system is that all processors are likely to be executing parts of the same program, whereas in a loosely coupled system each processor is likely to be executing its own programs.

Ada is not equally applicable to all forms of tightly coupled system. The more visible the multiprocessor architecture is to the Ada application developer, the less suited it is to the use of Ada. For example, if all the main store is shared, the run-time system may be able to load-share tasks across the processors; if only some storage is shared, special action is required when the program is built to ensure that code is executed from where its data can be accessed. This latter arrangement can require the imposition of design constraints coupled with the use of tools to configure programs in order to ensure the efficient use of the hardware. In an extreme case, it may not be possible for an Ada compilation system to enable the efficient use of the architecture.

15.3   Processing Power

Where multiple processors are required for increased processing power, the kind of system needed depends on just where that power is wanted. A general increase in power might be achieved by a load sharing, tightly coupled system. At the application programming level, the existence of multiple processors may not even be apparent, with the scheduling of the load being undertaken by a multiprocessor operating system. On the other hand, application system developers may be able to take advantage of the system structure by designing their application programs in such a way that there are clearly defined components which can be executed in parallel.

Increased power can also be obtained by the addition of processors for specialised functions. This is considered in section 15.8.

15.4 Economics

Economics in this context is a matter of matching power to cost. As suggested earlier, increased computing power can be obtained from a combination of processors. A combination of smaller processors may develop the same power as a larger, single processor, but yield cost savings for the right application. For example:

- for a loosely coupled system, simpler operating system software may be used, reducing system overheads;

- certain software may only need to be licenced for use on one of the smaller processors;

- maintenance of the less complex hardware may be cheaper;

- failure of a processor has only a degrading effect and reduces the need for a standby system.

If the application computer system adopted is loosely coupled, it may be possible to upgrade and enhance it piecemeal rather than having to replace the system as a whole. Application programs, and compilation systems in particular, need to be able to accommodate any resulting differences between the processors in the upgraded application computer system.

15.5 Flexibility

Where load sharing or parallel processing is possible, the performance of a system can depend on the number of processors employed. This has economic implications, but it also means that it may be possible to tailor system performance to the actual requirements of the operation. In general, the programming requirements are that it should be possible, by program design or otherwise, to take advantage of as many processors as are available. Thus there may need to be facilities in the compilation process or the run-time system to take account of differing numbers of processors.

15.6 Redundancy

Redundancy is provided in a system so that the failure of a component does not have a disastrous effect on the system as a whole. As was indicated earlier, a suitably structured, loosely coupled system may allow processors to be removed from the system and replaced without the need to stop the whole system. The same facility might also be provided

Multiprocessing

in a tightly coupled system, although the tightness of the coupling may often preclude this. In either case, some assistance at least is usually required from the underlying operating system or the support software, and generally some means whereby application programs can detect changes in configuration can be useful. For an application program to be able to take action, support in the compilation system is required.

15.7 Standby Facility

A standby facility is a special case of redundancy in that virtually the complete system is duplicated, although lesser amounts are possible. In the context of multiple processors, a standby processor is often described as being on warm or hot standby. The implication of these terms is that the secondary processor is linked to the primary processor in such a way that it is able to take over the primary role immediately. For hot standby, the secondary processor is shadowing the primary processor in all respects, maintaining its own set of data. Only its output is suppressed. For warm standby, the secondary processor may be performing some other task, but it has full access to the same data as the primary processor and may take over the primary role at a moment's notice.

The extent to which applications need to be aware of any change-over can vary, but particular requirements affecting a warm standby may be the need to recover from failed transactions, to validate the data left by the old primary processor, and to set up quickly any necessary complex structures, such as parallel tasks, on the second processor.

To a large extent the Ada language does not support the rapid restarting of a program, and therefore support from the run-time system is required to achieve this.

15.8 Specialisation

Not all processors are designed as general-purpose computing engines. Some are designed to be particularly efficient as, for example, communications processors, database machines, or array processors. By putting particular application's functions into appropriate processors, the overall efficiency of the application may be improved. The use of front-end communications processors for mainframes is now a classic example of this application of multiple processors.

Depending on the nature of the specialisations involved, some means is required either to direct the instructions of the program automatically to the appropriate processor, or else to assist the application developer to construct the software to take advantage of the different processors in the most efficient manner.

15.9 Distribution

A distributed system is essentially a loosely coupled system, and may consist of a variety of processors connected by some form of network. Each processor on the network is likely to be running its own programs. During development of the application system, there may be a common file store and, in particular, a common database to ensure the consistency of program and data interfaces. This might be reflected in the use of a common Ada program library where the various processors are compatible. The network may have one or more processors dedicated to program compilation, irrespective of the kinds of processors on the network.

15.10 Security

The ensuring of security within a computer system, that is, ensuring that sensitive data is not accessible to applications or parts of applications which have no right of access, is a complex and costly business, with much research and development work still to be done. Partitioning a system between multiple processors with trusted gateways in between is one way of reducing the complexity. Security is discussed in chapter 9 of this Guide.

15.11 Simplicity

An application which has a number of activities to be managed in parallel can place significant demands on the scheduling algorithms employed in a single processor system. Determining the relative priorities of the different tasks which must be performed can be an arduous exercise for the application designer, with practical demonstration being the only way to validate any design simulation.

Partitioning such a system between multiple processors can be an effective way of reducing the system's complexity at the possible expense of increasing the complexity of the program development tools.

15.12 Operational Considerations in a Multiprocessor System

Communication between processors in a multiprocessor system may be viewed at various levels. At the lowest level, mechanisms usually involve message channels or shared storage. Higher levels may provide the means of invoking services from separate processors, either synchronously, as a remote procedure call, or asynchronously as in a remote job activation.

Different kinds of control may be required over placement of tasks. The application system may allocate tasks to processors dynamically, or the allocation may be controlled statically by the application designer or dynamically by the end user.

The choice of software on each processor may be dictated by such factors as the manufacturer of the hardware, the specialisation of the processor, or the characteristics of the processor's configuration. Thus, data exchanged between processors may undergo various conversion processes on the way.

16

Use Of High Level Tools

In some applications, the Ada code which is submitted to the compilation system may have been produced through the use of a high-level tool. Such a tool might provide support for a design method such as MASCOT (Modular Approach to Software Construction, Operation and Test, Joint IECCA and MUF Committee, 1987) or SSADM, or it may be a fourth-generation language or application generator which takes a high-level statement of a requirement and produces an Ada program which meets that requirement. An example of the latter might be a database query system. Another example is a tool which takes a formal representation of a grammar for a programming language and generates a syntax analyser for the language. Two classes of problem may arise from the use of such tools: capacity and complexity problems and problems of language feature usage.

16.1 Capacity and Complexity Problems

Tools are capable of producing very large programs and may not check that their output is becoming too large for a compilation system to cope with. A tool can produce source code which is larger than a human writer may easily generate, or may contain very large or complex constructs: aggregates may be so large as to exceed the working space available for their construction; case statements may be so long as to render the mechanism used for their evaluation inefficient, or worse still may exceed the capabilities of the addressing mechanisms used in making the selection; expressions may be so complex as to exceed the temporary storage allowed for intermediate results.

Capacity limits of the Ada compilation system must be checked against those of the tool to ensure compatibility.

16.2 Language Feature Problems

A high-level tool may make use of Ada constructs in combinations which are unusual, or may rely on relatively complex parts of the language; for example one implementation of the MASCOT design method makes very heavy use of generics and tasking. This may result in errors in the Ada compilation system being encountered which do not appear in the course of normal, manual usage and have been missed in the supplier's testing procedures. Implementation features of the language supported by an Ada compilation system must be checked against those required by the tool to ensure compatibility.

If the generating tool is proprietary, it may not be possible to modify it to suit the compilation system. Further processing of its output may be possible, either manually or by a further tool, but is likely to be uneconomic in all but the simplest cases. Additionally, manual processing is likely to be impeded by the lack of intelligibility usually associated with mechanically generated code.

17

Training

17.1 Introduction

The training requirement imposes a significantly different set of parameters in the selection of an appropriate compilation system to that considered for a development or maintenance environment.

The training requirement can be the outcome of one of two training environments: the training organisation and the in-house training department of a development or maintenance organisation.

The training organisation is not limited to any particular hardware or operating system constraints. The compilation system can be chosen for the way it meets the training requirements without any external influences. The in-house training organisation can be supporting a spread of targets, projects, organisations and roles and hence a compromise must be achieved between satisfying the need for inclusion of specific features and ensuring that trainees gain an appreciation of general aspects, thus retaining a flexible training base.

The training environment is geared to support the employment needs of the trainees. Trainees may move onto one of several areas of software responsibility including senior management, project control and design tasks. This variety of trainee function causes different requirements to be placed on the compilation system.

17.2 The Training Requirements

The most important requirements are flexibility, multi-user support and the provision of diagnostic support. To a lesser extent there are the requirements of project support environment facilities, documentation and vendor support.

The compilation system needs to be flexible to provide, potentially, the opportunity of rehosting and retargeting. As the training environment matures; and the scope of training increases, limitations in the hardware configuration may become apparent. If a new hardware configuration is to be put into place then the cost of updating the training materials must be evaluated if the new hardware necessitates a significant change to the compilation system, for example a change of supplier. There could be a similar effect if enhancements are made to the hardware or operating system.

In a training environment it is important that the interactive facilities are suitable for students such that they do not interfere with the training process. Students' computer skills and quickness of learning vary so there may be a requirement to have variable interaction facilities that the student can select from. One difficulty in teaching Ada, although this is a greater difficulty for other languages, is to teach the Ada language as described in the Reference Manual without the inclusion of implementation dependent features. To aid this the compilation system may contain the facility to either reject code that uses implementation dependent features or at least provide a warning. In this way the trainee is made aware that the particular feature may not be available on all compilation systems.

The compilation system may be used by many trainees simultaneously as exercises are performed. It is probable that support is needed for up to fifteen simultaneous users who could be at different stages in the exercises, for example compiling, editing, linking or executing. The response time for a compilation is probably more important than the response time of the run-time system. This is due to the trainee repeatedly submitting their program for compilation as errors are traced and removed. However it is likely that the program is small and once it has been successfully compiled it does not require much time to execute.

Gaining experience from errors frequently contributes to the process of learning. It is therefore very important that the diagnostic support provides information in a clear and concise way so that the inexperienced user can quickly identify and correct errors. This requires the provision of:

- user selectable source listings, that is the amount of information provided in the source listing can be controlled by the user;
- compiler messages, that is clear indications of where errors are located;
- trace, cross-reference listings, and link and load reports, that is information about the mapping of the source code to the target address space;
- error message presentation, that is the message must be meaningful to the user providing clear information about the location and type of error and perhaps possible causes;
- source level debug, that is the ability to use the source code as the interface to the debugger and therefore be unconcerned about how the compilation system has optimised and allocated the code in the binary image;
- system usage statistics, that is to be able to monitor how much processing time, input and output requests, disk accesses the software is using during execution.

As Ada is a language for software engineers, other techniques are likely to be included in the training process, for example, the use of source code generators and design methodologies. It is therefore of benefit if the compilation system is part of a project support environment which contains tools providing these other functions. This may be through the provision of a tool interface specified in the public domain or the compilation system may be part of a proprietary environment.

The documentation of the compilation system must be comprehensible and meaningful to inexperienced users who are not only unfamiliar with the user interface to the compilation system but also with the Ada language. This is particularly important for the documentation of error messages as this is the most frequently used part of any manuals supplied.

Training environments can require that many users can access the system but the run-time system is unlikely to be used for any commercial benefit, for example it will not become part of an embedded system. This may lead to a different form of licensing agreement than for many development and maintenance environments.

Inexperienced users can write software that can severely test the compilation system's error recovery and reporting mechanism because such software had not been anticipated. Any errors in the compilation system can be found by the inexperienced user as they use the language in an unusual way. The support from the compilation system supplier needs to match these requirements, for example the use of a telephone hotline in case difficulties arise during a training course which must be resolved immediately in order for the course to progress.

PART II Questionnaires

18

Introduction To Part II

Part II of this Guide contains questions designed to provide information which is significant when choosing a compilation system. The questions are grouped into questionnaires, each covering a particular aspect of a compilation system. Advice on which aspects are of importance for any particular application is provided in Part I of the Guide.

Each questionnaire has an introduction followed by the set of questions. In some cases the questions are divided into subsections, each with its own introduction. For each question, information is given on how to interpret the different answers which may be received. The questions are directed at users of Ada compilation systems in different application areas and therefore reflect the level of detail required to make an informed choice. The Guide takes into account the effect of different implementation techniques the compilation system supplier may have adopted, but only describes these techniques where this gives an aid to understanding the benefits and problems that may arise.

19

Compilation System Facilities

19.1 Introduction

Despite the uniformity imposed upon Ada compilation systems by the language standard and the Ada validation test suite, compilation systems are still able to provide a wide variety of facilities which can be used to ease the development of Ada software. The set of facilities provided may be influenced by the man-machine interface of the compilation system, which is considered separately in its own questionnaire. However, there is also a dependence upon the underlying operating system and hardware.

The task of developing Ada software can be affected by the scope of the editor, debugging facilities and team working opportunities. The compilation system may provide tools which give assistance. However, the need for these tools depends upon the development environment, the method of working, the size of the software and the hardware configuration, and their importance varies from project to project.

19.2 The Development Environment

The environment for the development of Ada software can range from a small project team using a single computer as both host and target, to a multisite team developing software on a variety of hosts for a number of target systems. The size of the software under development and the expected lifetime for the software also influences the development facilities necessary for the project. Modern techniques for supporting the analysis, design and implementation stages of a development project tend to bring with them their own collections of tools. Whilst use of such techniques is by no means limited to the larger projects, in general it can be assumed that the larger the project and the longer the lifetime of the software under development, the greater are the number and sophistication of the facilities necessary for the development of the software. Tools to support specific development methods are outside the scope of this Guide.

Q19.2.1 Can compiled units be shared between Ada program libraries?

If the software is being developed by a large project team then it is probable that this team is divided into different sub-teams each involved in the development of particular functions of the software. The project might be organised such that each team or group of teams maintains its individual

Ada program library. Although the functions of the software under development by the sub-teams are different, software modules could be developed for use by more than one team, for example interrupt handlers. The software for the common utilities could usefully be stored in a single Ada program library which is accessed by the different teams when they are building their own Ada program sub-libraries. Without the ability to share a common copy of a utility, there is a danger that amendments are not incorporated in all parts of the developed software.

Another important advantage of the ability to share libraries is that tested modules may be kept in a frozen Ada program library. Other, dependent, software can use this library during development.

Q19.2.2 Is there support for partial linking?

During the development of software containing many modules it may be unnecessary to link all the modules of the software together in order to monitor or test particular parts of the software. Furthermore there may be resource constraints, such as the time required to do a full link, or the working space that needs to be allocated, which would discourage the inclusion of these unnecessary modules. The ability to link only part of the system could greatly ease any resource constraints there may be.

An additional benefit during the development of software occurs when modules of the software become stable, after having have been fully tested. It may be necessary to repeatedly relink these modules with other modules which are still at an earlier phase of development. If the stable modules can be partially linked into a unit then resources can be saved each time the revised system is linked, for example for further testing.

Q19.2.3 Does the program library provide facilities for variant and version control?

During the development of software of any size there is a need for the creation and use of variants and new versions of software modules already in the program library. A new version is created when modifications are made to a module and the modified module is to supersede the original module. A variant is created when modifications are made to a module and the modified module is to act as an alternative to the original module. There may be facilities provided in a compilation system to ease the creation and inclusion of new versions of software. There may also be facilities to ease the creation of variants of software modules and at a later date to remove them from the library, reclassify them as new versions, or reclassify them as new software modules. At all times it should be possible to identify individually the different versions and variants, and to trace back from a compiled version or variant of a module to the exact source code from which it was compiled. If the compilation system does not provide version and variant control, the application system developer needs to either devise a manual mechanism compatible with whatever is provided, or find some way of integrating the program library with any other control mechanism the software developer chooses to use.

Q19.2.4 What facilities does the compilation system supply for discretionary access control?

The facilities that need to be checked against requirements include the granularity of access control, the facilities for user groups and tool-based permissions, and the access control modes supported.

The access control of a unit may determine which program library the unit is stored in, if access control is applied only to the program library as a whole. If individual units or groups of units can have their own access control, then program libraries can be constructed more flexibly and conveniently.

For a large development it is convenient to be able to control access in terms of groups of users as well as individual users. Facilities are then needed for such groups to be set up and administered. It is also convenient if tools can be granted access rights as well as users, so that, for instance, a utility tool could read certain details of every unit in a program library.

Different modes of access need to be controlled separately. Obvious examples are to read, to write, and to execute, but many others are possible for instance to append but not overwrite, to annotate, and to read or write certain information only, for example dependences of units.

Q19.2.5 Does the compilation system support mandatory access control?

This is only required if the application is to handle classified information. The facilities required relate to the security rating required for the application system. This is a specialised subject which it would be inappropriate to pursue here.

Q19.2.6 What facilities are provided for configuration control?

The principal reason for wanting to hold more than one version or variant of a module in the program library is that it is required to build more than one version or variant of the application. Typically, during the development stages of an application, baseline versions are built which represent stable points in the progress towards each variant of the finished product. Modules which are parts of subsets of a complete system are developed beyond these baselines and, for testing purposes, give rise to different builds of the system. Several areas of the application may be developing in parallel, and tests in any of these areas may reveal faults in other parts of the system. A configuration management system enables the application developers to keep track of which versions of a module are used in each build of the system, and therefore to identify which builds are affected by a faulty module. It facilitates the building of new baselines from appropriate combinations of unchanged and revised modules, using proven versions of modules where the later versions have yet to meet their acceptance criteria.

Once the application is completed and released, further development may take place, perhaps as a result of user feed-back, leading to further releases. Additionally, yet more variants of the application may be required to meet the differing requirements of users. At any instant, then, there may be many different releases of the application in the field, and still others under development, each containing a different collection of versions and variants of the same software modules. It becomes impractical to maintain a separate program library for each release. Therefore configuration management facilities, closely coupled with the ability of the program library itself to hold multiple versions and variants, become essential if the application developer is to maintain control of the software modules throughout the life of the application.

Q19.2.7 Are there support facilities in the compilation system which make it particularly appropriate for use with any formalised development method?

It may be the case that, in some way, the compilation system supports the use of a particular development method. One of the most straightforward ways in which it could do this might be by the provision of a set of packages and subprograms. These might be in source form, or pre-compiled in a form which enables them to be imported into an Ada program library.

To take a specific example, a development method which is widely used in the programming of military systems in the United Kingdom is called MASCOT. In MASCOT, an application is subdivided into a collection of Activities which communicate through Intercommunication Data Areas known as Channels and Pools. To support developments using MASCOT, a compilation system might provide generic packages and subprograms as templates for Channels and Pools and for the primitives used to access them.

Q19.2.8 How is the target loaded?

The software may be developed on a host machine which has a good development environment, with many different facilities, but be executed on a bare target machine. The way the host and target machine communicate and hence the different possibilities for how the target software can be down-loaded can greatly influence software development. In the worse case

Compilation System Facilities

the software may have to be transferred using a separate medium, for example floppy disk, which is written by the host machine and read by the target machine. A generally more convenient system is a high-speed link between the two machines, with the target software being automatically downloaded in response to a command on the host machine. Part of the downloader usually resides on the target: this must not unduly limit the size of the target software that can be downloaded.

Q19.2.9 What facilities does the editor support?

It is becoming common practice for editors to be screen-oriented, and this is generally thought to lead to better productivity than line-oriented editors. Even more sophisticated are structured editors, which impose a structure on the text being edited, one example being syntax-driven editors which incorporate a knowledge of Ada syntax. These are sometimes thought to be more suitable for beginners than those having experience of the language.

The basic facilities needed for development of software are insert, search, cut-and-paste, delete, and replace. More specialised features are syntax checking, which detects syntax errors of complete or incomplete units before compilation; some of the features of a word processor, for example to assist laying out extensive comments; and macro facilities, allowing application developers to tailor the editor to their own needs.

This issue is also a matter of the man-machine interface. See chapter 24, Man-Machine Interface.

Q19.2.10 What facilities does the debugger support for host systems?

In a perfect world software would be developed without errors and so a debugger would be unnecessary. However in this world debuggers are needed to establish why software is not performing as designed, and as the reasons for errors are manifold, so a powerful debugger is an aid to productivity. Typical of the facilities required of a debugger are setting breakpoints in the program, tracing the course of execution of program statements, and monitoring and resetting the values of program variables. Useful facilities specific to Ada are monitoring of the states of tasks, and monitoring the raising and handling of exceptions.

To be useful a debugger should communicate with the user in terms of the source program, and not the compiled code. Debuggers are most often used interactively, but it can be useful to be able to use a debugger in batch mode as a monitor during testing.

Q19.2.11 What facilities does the debugger support for host-target systems?

When the software is actually executed on a target system then the facilities on the target system, for example the existence of input and output devices, greatly influence how the software can be debugged. The facilities identified in question Q19.2.9 are still applicable but they may not be feasible because the target configuration has no input or output devices, not even to the host. There are three scenarios for debugging and they are described in performance order.

- The target may have sufficient facilities for debugging to take place directly on the target without any further recourse to the host system.

- The software executing on the target is debugged via commands from the host, the output may be directed to the host or produced by the target directly.

- The target may have no debugging facilities and code inserts are required. That is there is no debugging tool available for the target so additional code must be added to output important variables at critical points.

All debugging facilities, and their possible complexities, have performance implications on real-time software.

19.3   Run-time Aspects

The compilation system can provide facilities which are relevant to the run time system.

Q19.3.1 What facilities does the compilation system provide to enable the application system developer to control the location in store of program code and data?

There are various reasons for wanting to control the location of code and data. For example, in an embedded control system, it is common practice to retain program code in read-only memory (ROM), whereas, of necessity, variable data must be held in writable store (RAM). The target architecture and application considerations may define the different address ranges which must be used for ROM and RAM, and thus it becomes essential for the compilation system to provide adequate means of control.

Further examples of the need for such a facility include:

- keeping heavily used code and data in faster storage;

Compilation System Facilities

- where only some of the store is accessible to more than one processor in a multiprocessor configuration, ensuring that code and data that must be shared are held in shared store;

- ensuring that code and data which must be kept secure are located in the designated secure parts of the computer;

- when only some of the RAM has battery back-up power, arranging that data which must be preserved during a power failure is located there.

The Ada language provides address clauses for the application system developer to use to control where code and data are located, but compilation system suppliers are not obliged to implement this feature of the language. It is also permissable for a compilation system to have facilities in, for example, the linker to provide very powerful location controls which enable the application system developer to revise the target store layout without changing the Ada source code.

Q19.3.2 How does the compilation system facilitate the execution of code on multiprocessor targets?

A multiprocessor target architecture can have a significant impact on the run-time performance of an application, and this can be a negative impact if there is a poor match between the facilities the run-time system provides and the needs of the application. Depending on the architecture, the compilation system may need to take special action for any interaction between processes executing code on different processors, whether this be for a rendezvous, shared data, or a remote procedure call. The facilities offered have to be examined directly in relation to the features of the target and the needs of the application. There are further questions relating to multiprocessor targets in Chapter 22, Run-Time Implementation Concerns.

Q19.3.3 To what extent does the compilation system take account of the facilities available on the target?

It is usually the case that a target may have optional features which are only provided when necessary. For example, a target rarely has all the storage it is capable of addressing. Targets are often only supplied with floating point processors when they are expected to perform a significant amount of floating point processing, the application system developer otherwise being prepared to accept floating point operations performed by software. For economic or other reasons, a compilation system supplier may decide to direct the product at a common denominator, with the result that, for example, even when a floating point processor is available, it is ignored and software routines are used instead. Thus the application system developer should identify those target options which are important to the application and establish that they are fully supported by the compilation system.

19.4 Maintenance Facilities

The maintenance of any software can be a cumbersome and unfulfilling task if the facilities are inadequate. Good software engineering practice during the design phases can also make a great difference to the effectiveness of maintenance, so the compilation system facilities which allow or encourage this are relevant here.

Q19.4.1 Does the compilation system report any use of implementation-dependent facilities in the source code it is processing?

A compilation system can implement various pragmas and other implementation-defined facilities which could cause the software to require minor modifications if it is ported to another configuration or to another compilation system for the same configuration. This can cause difficulties if the software is moved to a new configuration because of a hardware upgrade or if a compilation system is no longer supported. Although the unregulated use of implementation-dependent features should normally be discouraged, they may be necessary to exploit a required feature of the processor, and so it is beneficial for their use to be highlighted.

Q19.4.2 Can non-adherence to coding standards be monitored?

Maintenance of software is greatly eased if the software is readable and understandable and conforms to a coding standard agreed within an organisation or software section. It may be possible to inform the compilation system of the standard so that it may monitor any non-adherence to the standard. Examples of coding standards are the appearance of comments at defined places, the absence of goto statements, and procedure end identifiers. Further information about good Ada coding style is given in Portability and Style in Ada (Nissen and Wallis, 1984)

Q19.4.3 Does the compilation system provide facilities for variant and version control?

This question has already been discussed in section 19.2. During the maintenance period modifications are made to units and new versions and variants are tried within a tested system.

Q19.4.4 What is the documentation support from the compilation system?

The compilation system can provide facilities which help the maintenance of the software by the use of documentation aids during the development and subsequent updating of the software. The use of cross-reference listers and source formatters can help in the creation of adequate documentation which is even more important in the maintenance phase. A library manager may also provide facilities to describe the contents of the library.

Another facility is the enforced documentation of changes. This might be imposed by the editor, checked as part of the coding standard, or be tied in to version and variant control.

20

Quality and Documentation

20.1 Introduction

There is no universally agreed measure of quality: there is always a subjective element in such a judgement, and various aspects are of more or less importance in different applications. This questionnaire identifies issues which are of general importance and raises others which are more specific. There is a natural tendency when evaluating a product to aim for the highest possible quality but in reality the product's quality need only to be sufficient to satisfy its requirement. The required level of quality for the application system must first be determined, therefore; this questionnaire can then be used to suggest questions to ask the compilation system supplier and to interpret the responses in determining if the compilation system will enable those requirements to be met.

20.2 The Compilation System Supplier

The experience of the compilation system supplier can provide some indication of the likely quality of the product. This is not to discount the new supplier in the market place but quality indicators are based on more information when the experience of the supplier is greater.

The supplier's policies and practices on timely correction of errors and assurance that errors do not reoccur are of particular importance.

Q20.2.1 Has the compilation system supplier developed a number of compilation systems, not necessarily for Ada?

The experience gained from solving compilation system issues previously, even for other languages, under the relevant operating system family, may be expected to show improvement in the quality of the product in question.

Q20.2.2 Can the compilation system supplier demonstrate a satisfied customer base?

An introduction to previous customers with whom independent contact can be made is the best method of assessing how well the product has been received. Other customers can give views on how close they consider the product is to its intent and how accurate the pre-sale literature is. The compilation system supplier may be able to provide written references from satisfied customers and these could be followed up by making direct contact. This approach may be taken up to obtain confirmation of the answers to any of the following questions.

Q20.2.3 Has the supplier official quality accreditation?

Accreditation may be desirable or mandatory, depending on the policy of the end-user. Examples are accreditation to the International Standard ISO 9000 (British Standards Institution standard BS5750), and military accreditation to NATO AQAP-1 (Allied Quality Assurance Publication 1) standards.

Q20.2.4 Given that a significant error is reported, seriously delaying or completely inhibiting the customer's progress, how long would the supplier take to fix it?

As an Ada compilation system is a complex item of software, one must expect, and plan to deal with, the presence of errors. The supplier is in a difficult position since it is not always possible to predict the effort required to fix an error. Hence the supplier may not give a simple, direct answer to the question; the application system developer has to judge how helpful the reply is. The application system developer should seek a response commensurate with any maintenance fee for the compilation system. For example, it might be expected that the supplier would offer a service whereby, as an initial step, advice would be given on how to avoid the problem so that progress could be resumed as soon as possible. This might be followed up with regular progress reports on solving the problem, with predictions of when the correction would be released to users.

Q20.2.5 Given any error, how long would it take before a compilation system is released without it?

The previous question dealt with specific customer support, while this one addresses general support for the compilation system.
As part of the mechanism to ensure that compilation systems adhere to the standard for the language, there is a suite of validation test programs and a number of authorities who validate candidate compilation systems against this suite before issuing certificates of validity; see Introduction. As the validation test suite has developed towards maturity, so the policies of the validation authorities have changed. Thus, the period for which a certificate is issued has increased as the test suite has stabilised. The policy, at the time of writing this Guide, is that a validation certificate must be renewed after a specific period.

Quality and Documentation

It can never be assumed that the validation test suite detects all errors, although attempts are made to incorporate appropriate tests whenever a new kind of error is identified.

Another aspect of current policy is that the suite is frozen some time before it comes into force so that compilation system suppliers have a chance to correct any errors detected by the suite before they have to submit their compilation systems to formal testing.

A consequence of these policies is that any error in a compilation system should, sooner or later, be corrected if the compilation system is to maintain its validated status. The longest that a known error can be allowed to survive depends on just when it was discovered (and publicised) relative to releases of the validation test suite. This could be of the order of years.

A release of a compilation system which the supplier affirms only corrects faults does not need to be revalidated ahead of the renewal date of its existing certificate. Therefore it is pertinent to expect the supplier to adopt a policy of making additional releases of the compilation system to correct known faults. For inexpensive compilation systems a new release may have to be paid for as a special item, while for other compilation systems, a regular maintenance agreement may be required. Revalidation takes time and effort, and hence some cost is inevitable.

Q20.2.6 Are all tests which demonstrate errors in a previous release of a compilation system rerun on each new release to show that the new release clears all the old errors?

Checking that old errors do not recur in new releases is called regression testing. It is a standard software engineering method aimed at ensuring a good quality product. A compilation system supplier might be expected to build up a collection of tests which have demonstrated problems in the past, and to run these tests against new versions of the compilation system before the new versions are released. This should ensure that faults corrected by earlier releases have not been reintroduced by the latest set of corrections or improvements.

20.3   Maturity of the Compilation System

There are a number of questions which can be asked about the maturity of the compilation system. It is still a feature of software products that the more they are used the greater the probability that errors originally present in the software will have been discovered and removed, although others could have been introduced. However, a compilation system supplier may go some way towards minimising the number of undiscovered errors through the use of effective testing techniques during product development, maybe with the assistance of tools based on formal methods. Evidence of the compilation system maturity is given by the following indicators.

Q20.3.1 What is the current version number of the compilation system, how many releases have there been, and over what period?

A large number of releases gives an indication, either that the product has been well tested by users or that many errors have been found. The period over which the releases have been made is an indication of the stability of the product. Thus many releases over a long period is a promising sign. If the history of releases is unavailable, some indication of the number of releases that have been made can be gained from the version number of the latest release, although this can be misleading as some numbers may not have been used, and some releases may not have been given completely new version numbers.

Q20.3.2 When was the last error reported? How many errors are waiting to be corrected in the next version release? When was the last error corrected? In total how many errors have been reported since the compilation system has been publicly available?

The answers to these questions could give an assessment of the frequency with which errors are found in the compilation system. The supplier may only be willing to release the information to certain types of customers. It is sensitive information which only confident suppliers may be willing to release. It should be borne in mind that, however, there may be other justifiable reasons for not releasing the information.

Q20.3.3 Has the compilation system been moved to another host configuration either by the compilation system supplier or by a third party?

When a compilation system is moved to a new environment, latent errors may be exposed which are typically associated with assumptions about the environment made during the initial development. The correction of the parent compilation system for these errors can increase its robustness when it is required for new application environments which may exercise previously less well tested facilities.

Q20.3.4 Has the compilation system been used on large and lengthy projects, and for compiling complex programs?

A compilation system that has already been used for a large or lengthy project is likely to have received much more severe use than a system

Quality and Documentation

which has been used only for demonstrations, for example. Additionally, another application developer who has selected and used a compilation system in this way is likely to have already put pressure on the compilation system supplier to ensure that all important errors detected are corrected.

20.4 The Robustness of the Compilation System

Statistical methods of measuring reliability can be applied to software, but at the time of writing they are only rough indicators. The maturity of the compilation system, as addressed in the previous section, gives an indication of the compilation system's reliability and the following questions aim to determine its robustness, a closely linked measurement.

Q20.4.1 How is the robustness of the compilation system measured?

A compilation system can be tested by the use of tests generated by experienced personnel to achieve a degree of robustness appropriate to everyday use. However, such testing does not generally stress the compilation system in all ways that it may be used. For example, if the application developer uses software engineering tools or methods which automatically generate Ada source code, or result in large numbers of units, limitations in the compilation system may be brought to light which would not otherwise be apparent. The following are related questions to the measurement of robustness.

Q20.4.2 Is the compilation system self-compiled?

An Ada compilation system is itself a very complex program, and many Ada compilers are written using Ada. If the compilation system is used to compile and maintain itself, that is a good indication that, in many areas at least, the compilation system is capable of handling complex programs.

Q20.4.3 Has the compilation system been developed for the development of software using only one particular technique, for example Object Oriented Design or MASCOT?

The structure of the software and the size of modules vary according to the development method used. It is therefore possible that the compilation system may have limitations which are acceptable for the method it has been developed for, but may be unacceptable for the method the application developer is considering.

20.5 The Scope of the Compilation System

Although commercially available Ada compilation systems have passed the validation test suite there is still scope for variation between the features a compilation system offers because the standard identifies some items as implementation dependent.

Q20.5.1 Is the Validation Summary Report available for inspection?

The Validation Summary Report is available from the Ada Validation Facility which validated the compilation system. However the compilation system supplier may provide copies to prospective customers upon request, thus minimising delays in acquiring a copy. The validation summary report, as well as describing the validation process for a particular compilation system, also lists the way the implementation-dependent features have been implemented. These are given in an Appendix to the document and so are easily identified. Throughout the questionnaires in this Guide reference is made to these implementation-dependent features, and the Validation Summary Report is an authoritative document which identifies them.

Q20.5.2 How is the compilation system limited by the hardware or operating system?

Although validated Ada compilation systems may not support supersets or subsets of Ada, there may be limitations on how much of the language standard is implemented because of hardware or operating system constraints. These are usually identified in the Validation Summary Report because they cause tests to be inapplicable but their reporting is not so readily accessible as the implementation-dependent features. Most compilation systems for the same configuration have similar limitations but there may be some suppliers who have found alternative solutions to provide increased functionality. These allowable differences can result in the production of software which is not portable and which cannot be re-used with different compilation systems and should be taken into account when designing any Ada software.

20.6 The Development Scenario

The compilation systems available vary significantly in the methods of working they support. These differences are not directly performance issues of the run-time system, which are considered in chapter 22, Run-Time Implementation Concerns, but they affect the way a software development team can use the compilation system and the resources that the compilation system requires.

Quality and Documentation 85

Q20.6.1 What is contained in the user documentation?

The compilation system may be excellent and offer good error tracking facilities, but if the user documentation is poor then the full potential of the compilation system may not be realised. Good user documentation contains, as a minimum:

- general guidance on use of the compilation system;

- instructions on how to run the compilation system;

- explanations of options and parameters;

- a run-time system description;

- a description of the organisation of the program at run time, especially type mapping.

An additional feature which improves the accessibility of the user documentation is a sample program which can be used when familiarisation with the compilation system takes place.

Q20.6.2 How extensive is the detection of run-time errors at compile time?

The compilation system may be able to identify some cases of erroneous programs during the compilation phase, for example the use of uninitialised variables.

Q20.6.3 Are the error messages generated during compilation?

The quality of error messages generated must be assured, although it is a feature difficult to prove. The error message must always be accurate. It is preferable to state the cause of error to be unknown than to indicate incorrectly the part of the language definition the program contravenes. The level of detail required of an error message depends on the skill level of the user and the application area. Some compilation systems provide alternatives for users with different levels of experience: a brief message and a descriptive message. There should be no penalties to the use of descriptive messages, unless space is critical.

Q20.6.4 How many users of the compilation system can there usefully be at one time?

Compilation times are artificially extended if the application system is to be developed using a software development team which expects to share Ada program libraries, and the compilation system permits only one user at a time to access a program library. This is particularly relevant where utility code for the application system is held in a single program library.

Q20.6.5 Does the compilation system exclude from the program it builds all code and data that is never accessed?

One of the major benefits of Ada is the use of packages. However if only one subprogram is to be used from a package then it is wasteful, and has performance disadvantages, for the whole package to be included in the code produced by the compilation system.

Q20.6.6 Are there any limitations on the size of the software components which can be included?

The use of external packages, for example mathematical libraries, may mean the inclusion of large components during compilation. The size of these components is not under the control of the application developer and may exceed the capacity of some compilation systems.

Q20.6.7 Is partial loading available?

Ada programs can assume considerable size, and the time taken to load a large program on to a target processor can be considerable. Additionally problems may arise during the loading process which require restarting. Therefore it is convenient if the object program can be segmented by the compilation system and loaded in separate parts. This facility is also useful if parts of the program have to be stored in ROM and only the RAM parts loaded.

20.7 Machine and Environment Facilities

The host and target machines and environments impose limitations upon the compilation system and object programs, but these limitations may be overcome to a greater or lesser extent by the compilation system. For suitable questions see the questionnaires on Performance and Capacity, Man-Machine Interface and Compilation System Facilities, chapters 21, 24 and 19 respectively.

Quality and Documentation

20.8 Security of the Program Library

Protection of the software under development requires attention not only to the source code but also to the Program Library. The limitations on access to contents of the library when using the compilation system are also critical.

Q20.8.1 Is the compilation system part of a high security system and if so what is its rating?

The United States Department of Defense has issued a set of definitions giving ratings for the security precautions which may be enforced (Trusted Computer System Evaluation Criteria, DoD Computer Security Center, 1983). These are frequently referred to as the Orange Book security definitions. The highest security rating is A1 and the lowest is D. The application for which the compilation system is required may have security requirements placed upon it by the customer which may be expressed in terms of the Orange Book definitions. It is not only the security rating of the compilation system that should be of concern, but also the extent to which the compilation system assists in ensuring that the application system is adequately secure.

Q20.8.2 Is the security offered by the compilation system provided by the operating system?

If security features are provided by the operating system then the security rating of the operating system must be investigated.

Q20.8.3 What security mechanisms are used?

Two examples of methods which help provide security are the use of encrypted code and the overwriting of returned data storage with a random bit pattern. The former mechanism helps prevent the code being easily interpreted if unauthorised access is obtained. The latter prevents the compilation system using pages of memory that contains information from a previous compilation which could then be reconstructed by an unauthorised user. Where Orange Book security is not required but where nevertheless there is a need to maintain confidentiality, it may be pertinent to identify all the measures that have been taken by the supplier of the compilation system to ensure that some level of security can be achieved. Although a useful rule may be that the more measures taken the better, a supplier should be able to justify the approach in terms of the threats to security against which it is protecting.

20.9 Run-Time Error Detection

How errors at run time are handled is an important aspect of a compilation system. Ada provides for the controlled trapping of some errors by the use of exception handlers, but there are a number of ways in which implementations may differ significantly.

Q20.9.1 How are unhandled exceptions catered for?

If a run-time exception occurs for which the program contains no handler, the language definition requires that the part of the program in which the exception was raised be terminated without any kind of reporting. However, during program development, it is useful to have such exceptions reported. The quality of error messages for unhandled exceptions is critical to the timely resolution of the error. Cryptic explanations or incorrect cause identification can be more destructive to problem solving than the absence of any error message.

Q20.9.2 Does detection of an expression which must raise an exception on evaluation give rise to a compile-time warning?

It is specifically recommended by the Reference Manual that a compiler should give a warning in such a case, as it usually indicates an error in the program.

Q20.9.3 Which cases of erroneous execution and incorrect order dependences are detected?

The language-defined exception PROGRAM_ERROR may, but need not be, raised by erroneous execution or incorrect order dependence. Not all such occurrences can be detected, even in theory, but the number of such cases detected is indicative of the quality of the compilation system.

Q20.9.4 Are system errors detected?

During the execution of an application system, it is possible that system errors may occur, either as a result of inherent faults in the compilation system, or because the application developer suppressed some run-time checks. Typical examples of system errors are attempts to execute an illegal instruction, attempts to access storage which is either nonexistent or has the wrong form of protection, or the failure of some consistency check in the run-time system. Although in many applications a system error may be disastrous and an adequate reaction is for the system to stop, other application systems are required to be resilient and to recover, a particular example being an operating system. Such systems require that the run-

Quality and Documentation

time system report the problem to the application software so that some action can be taken. For example, if the run-time system can detect that the application program itself has not been corrupted, it might raise an exception. Where the problem is more severe, it might raise a software interrupt which is handled by software in ROM to reload and restart the application system.

Q20.9.5 How do implementation-dependent features affect the exceptions raised?

The conditions under which certain exceptions are raised are implementation-dependent. An example of this is whether the run-time system can detect machine floating-point overflow.

Q20.9.6 What environmental events can the run-time system handle?

Q20.9.7 What environmental events can be passed to a program to handle?

Q20.9.8 After a power failure, can a program be restarted from the point of interruption, or must it be re-elaborated?

Under operational conditions, even a faultless program may encounter environmental influences which could cause incorrect operation. Whilst it is difficult to consider any standard form of recovery after a major malfunction, it may well be useful to look for intelligent responses to certain kinds of intermittent fault. For example, a momentary fluctuation in the power supply might result in the detection of a spurious store parity error. Operating systems often provide for retries in such cases, but an Ada program has to rely on the run-time system provided for it. Broadly, three classes of action by the run-time system are possible:

- stop the computer;

- handle the event internally as far as possible, hiding it from the program;

- cause an interrupt or raise an exception (possibly implementation defined) in the program.

20.10 Integrity of the Program Library

Maintaining the integrity of the program library is necessary to help ensure the correctness of the software under development. It is possible for the Ada compilation system to take a number of actions to help prevent this integrity from being diminished.

Q20.10.1 Is a transaction mechanism in use?

If changes to the program library are made using a transaction mechanism and for any reason the change is not completed, the program library is returned to its initial state before the transaction commenced. In this way the integrity of the program library is maintained because either all the changes are made or none of the changes are made.

The definition of a transaction may vary between different suppliers of compilation systems which could affect the maintenance of integrity. If the compilation system takes as a transaction a series of related changes as determined by the system, then it is more likely that integrity is maintained than if it takes as a transaction only a single change concerning one module in a sequence of linked changes.

Q20.10.2 Is there a backup mechanism for the program library?

It is quite probable that actions are incorrectly taken which causes the program library to be in error. If changes to the program library automatically cause the previous version to be overwritten then it is very time consuming to re-establish the library in its previous state, that is before the error took place. However if there is always a backup copy of the program library maintained then errors can be quickly cancelled by reverting to the backup version.

21

Performance and Capacity

21.1　Introduction

Performance and capacity can be thought of as the dynamic and static aspects of a single characteristic, which may be called capability. Each applies both to the development environment (compile time) and to the developed application (run time).

There are essentially two ways of obtaining information about a compilation system's capability: to measure and to ask.

To measure capability needs benchmarks: standard activities for the system to perform. For example, a capacity test would be to run the system with a different number of users doing fixed tasks. Performance tests consisting of timed loops of instructions are well known. This Guide is not concerned chiefly with benchmarks, although they are discussed in chapter 29, Benchmarks; but the following points may be made.

- A number of benchmarks are available, mostly for measuring run-time speed. Often the compilation system supplier is willing to provide the results of some (perhaps carefully selected) benchmarks. The results need interpreting with a great deal of care.

- The compilation system supplier may be willing to run a benchmark provided by the application system developer or to provide the compilation system for evaluation by the application system developer. In either case the conditions of running the benchmark need to be carefully controlled.

- The benchmark used needs to be closely matched to the anticipated application and development environment. If no such benchmark is available one can be written specially, but this is not a trivial task and needs to be approached seriously; the outcome can have profound effects throughout the lifetime of the development.

The rest of this chapter considers the second means of obtaining information: by asking the supplier questions about various aspects of the compilation system's capability.

21.2 Compile-time capability

To a greater or lesser extent a development can adapt to meet the capacity of the development system and, though less easily, to its performance; but too great a mismatch must be avoided. The following questions suggest some capacity features that might be of importance.

Q21.2.1 What is the largest compilation unit that can be compiled?

It is difficult to give a precise answer to this question, but it is important to know at least the order of magnitude. This is generally given in terms of lines of source code; this should be qualified to some extent by the sparseness of the lines, and whether blank lines and comment lines are included. There may also be a limit on the generated code size.

These limits can sometimes be overcome by splitting packages and using subunits, but this may be difficult or impossible in some cases. The size of compilation units is not always under the application developer's control, for example with bought-in software.

Q21.2.2 What language features, if any, significantly affect the answer to the previous question?

Examples of possible answers are:

- a large number of dependences, direct or indirect;

- the use of generic instantiation or in-line expansion of subprograms may increase the size of the unit;

- the use of optimisation may have an effect one way or the other by affecting the size of the generated code;

- the use of large data structures may give rise to hidden initialisations.

Q21.2.3 What system features, if any, affect the answer to question Q21.2.1?

The likeliest answer is the amount of main store (real or virtual) available to the compilation system; perhaps a simple formula can be given. Other possible answers are the amount of filestore available, and the system configuration if for example the compiler is configurable with different numbers of passes.

Q21.2.4 What other limits are there on the use of language features?

Some compilers allocate separate areas for particular intermediate data structures, and so place limits on language features quite apart from limits on total compilation size. In other cases a limit arises from the use of a fixed size of data item to hold a count or a number or other data associated with each object of some class. Examples are:

- the depth of nesting of program units (blocks, subprograms, packages and tasks) and compound statements;

- the number of enumeration literals in an enumeration type;

- the number of parameters to a subprogram;

- the number of discriminants in a record type;

- the number of dimensions of an array type;

- the size of an aggregate;

- the number of exceptions in a compilation unit;

- the number of library units referenced;

- the number of subprograms in a package;

- the number of choices in a case statement;

- the number of characters in a line;

- the number of exception handlers in a unit.

Q21.2.5 What is the maximum number of library units that can be held in the program library?

Often the program library is structured as a set of sub-libraries, so that this question should be asked of an individual sub-library and of the entire library. The number of library units in an Ada system should not be underestimated; even a medium-sized program can run into several thousand units.

Q21.2.6 What limits does the development system impose on the size of the object program?

Such limits can arise from various parts of the compilation system and be expressed in various ways. For instance, the linker may impose a limit on the number of compilation units that can be linked to form a program; partial linking may be provided to overcome this. The loader may impose a limit on the size of the program overall or various parts of it. Less definite limits may occur through performance issues, for example increase in linking time with number of compilation units.

Q21.2.7 How fast is the compiler?

This is perhaps the one question that every potential customer asks and every supplier is prepared to answer. It is also easy to measure provided the conditions are well-defined for example known machine configuration with no other jobs running. A common form of answer gives an overhead figure, plus so much per line of source text.

It is difficult to give any guidance here as to the answers to be expected as technology changes so rapidly, but asking other Ada users should give a good idea of what to expect. Ada compilers run rather more slowly than compilers for most languages because of the greater complexity of the language, especially the greater amount of checking that is done at compile time. Benchmarks are particularly useful here, but must be of a reasonable size: not less than about 1000-2000 lines, and preferably larger if the compiler can handle a unit of that size.

As with question Q21.2.1, the answer may be affected by system features such as the available main store, and by language features such as in-line expansion of subprograms and context clauses. Also the use of system options such as debugging, when the compilation system may need to generate extra information, and special listings, may affect the answer.

The efficiency of other parts of the compilation system can also be important; for example the linker can dominate in some kinds of development.

Q21.2.8 Can recompilation costs be reduced?

The powerful static checking features of Ada, while reducing overall development costs, tend to increase the number of recompilations. Careful management of the development process can help, but the compilation system can provide further relief. For example:

- It may provide assistance in choosing the most economical order of recompilation.

Performance and Capacity

- It may avoid unnecessary recompilation, for example of a unit dependent on another unit which has been changed in a way not affecting this unit.

Q21.2.9 How many users can the compilation system support at the same time?

The compilation system supplier and the application system developer may have quite different views on what is an acceptable level of support, and therefore it is important that this question be asked against a well defined specification. Such a specification should define not only the machine resources available, but should also define other characteristics in a realistic manner. For example, in a typical application development environment, only a proportion of the users are likely to be compiling Ada source code at any one time; others may be editing source, linking, testing, and writing documentation. It is important to establish the likely mixes of activities, and then to decide what is an acceptable level of performance for each mix considered. Performance might be expressed in terms of the rate at which lines of code are compiled, and the time taken to link a program of a specified size. Whatever metrics are used for performance, the application system developer should ensure that they are adequately defined and can be applied.

Some of the factors which can affect the number of users adequately supported are covered by the following questions.

Q21.2.10 Does the compiler operate a multipass system?

Even if the compiler is not re-entrant, if it is multipass then the whole compiler need not be present in a user's store. This reduces the amount of store required to support more than one user of the system at once. The same consideration may apply to other tools of the compilation system, for instance the linker.

Q21.2.11 How many users can share the same copy of the Ada standard packages?

If each user needs a copy of the Ada standard packages then the number of simultaneous users that can be supported is further limited by the amount of store available.

21.3 Run-time Capability

Q21.3.1 How big is the generated code?

An expansion ratio might be quoted: so many bytes per line of source. This is useful as an order of magnitude but no critical sizing should be based on it. For more accurate answers, benchmarks or specific questions related to the application in hand are essential. Besides typical values, maximum values might be of interest if they are guaranteed.

Q21.3.2 How much space on the target is taken by the compilation system?

Several parts of the compilation system might need space on the target:

- the run-time system;

- the target loader;

- the debugger.

This may be user-controllable to some extent; for example different versions of the run-time system are often available, with and without support for tasking or input-output.

Q21.3.3 What limits are there on the program at run-time?

There could be limits on the overall program size, perhaps not entirely dependent on the target size. There could also be limits on the size or number of specific features. Examples are:

- the number of tasks queued at an entry, or active in total;

- the depth of dynamic nesting of subprogram calls;

- the size of individual data items such as arrays;

- total size of code, local variable storage (stack), variables created by allocators (heap), and library package data.

The code size limit and code speed may be affected by suppression of run-time checks.

Q21.3.4 How fast is the generated code?

Here a general answer, in milliseconds per line of source text perhaps, is of little value, and specific questions or benchmarks are required. Typical and maximum values can be requested; if the application has critical timing constraints then predictability of timing, for instance by assured maximum values, is vital.

Performance and Capacity

Q21.3.5 How predictable is the timing?

Examples of factors which impair the predictability are:

- automatic garbage collection, that is a process that is invoked by the run-time system, either intermittently or when free storage is becoming short, to recover allocated storage which is no longer in use;

- storage allocation that proceeds in large amounts, so that a system call is required to acquire a new amount every so often.

If these effects exist it may be possible to allow for them, provided that enough information is available.

Q21.3.6 How efficient is the run-time system?

The principal areas of interest are:

- tasking: the time taken to create and activate a task, and to initiate and terminate a rendezvous;

- storage allocation: the time taken to evaluate an allocator;

- exceptions: the time taken to raise an exception, and any overhead caused by the presence of exception handlers.

Q21.3.7 What space overhead does tasking involve?

The run-time kernel can be somewhat simplified for an Ada program which consists of a single task. This is of particular relevance if space is at a premium.

There may be a fixed amount of store used by the run-time routines plus additional per-task space for scheduler tables. It is also quite likely that a compilation system does not optimise for a program which is a single task, and therefore there are no space savings to be had.

Q21.3.8 What is the algorithm to compute the proportion of time spent in the scheduler?

If an Ada program involves multiple tasks, there can be a significant amount of work for the scheduler to decide which task to run.

In practice, such an algorithm is likely to be complex, and an approximate rule of thumb has to be accepted. Such a rule might be based on the number of tasks, whether or not they are active, and the mean time between scheduling points such as rendezvous. Tasks waiting on select statements can introduce additional scheduling overheads, and therefore it might be expected that this would be reflected in the algorithm.

Q21.3.9 Are there any external effects of the run-time system?

This question relates to the interface between the program and its environment. Examples of interest are:

- Is it possible to prevent critical parts of the program from being swapped out of main store?

- Can compile time be traded against run time, for example in elaboration of static data?

See chapter 22, Run-Time Implementation Concerns for more examples.

Q21.3.10 What optimisations are performed by the compilation system?

It should not be a concern to the application system developer what optimisations are performed by the compiler. In fact, it is often difficult to draw a line between well generated code and optimised code. Nevertheless, it may be the sign of a well engineered product that the compilation system developer can provide a list of optimisations. Probably what is more of interest and value to the application system developer is knowing whether or not it is possible to gain some advantage from the optimisations. Therefore a simple list of optimisations needs to be accompanied by descriptions of the circumstances in which they apply, and any factors which inhibit the optimisations. Such a set of descriptions should enable an application system developer to evolve a set of good coding practices for the particular compilation system.

22

Run-Time Implementation Concerns

22.1 Introduction

The run-time characteristics of an Ada compilation system are of paramount importance for many applications, particularly those with a real-time element. At the same time the characterisation of those aspects of the run-time system which are of importance may be very difficult, particularly for users new to Ada systems.

Q22.1.1 What information is available about the robustness of the run-time system?

The supplier should maintain, and may make available, a log of all run-time system errors. If this information is available it will probably be in the form of a summary of known errors and outstanding problems which may or may not include information on the dates of errors. Where dates are given, perhaps only to very serious enquirers, the information may be used to determine the rate of discovery and solution of run-time system errors.
A full analysis of this information also requires information on the usage of the compilation system, which may be difficult to obtain.

Q22.1.2 Does the run-time system include a garbage collector and if so how does it operate and can its operation be modified by the user?

If a garbage collector is provided then in most cases it operates synchronously with respect to the rest of the Ada program, that is when it is invoked all other program activity must be suspended until the collection process is complete. This can lead to unexpected unpredictability of operation of programs.
If a garbage collector is provided there may be options available to the user to inhibit or otherwise control its operation.

Q22.1.3 What facilities are provided by the run-time system for interaction between distinct programs?

Over and above the standard Ada features for intra-program communication such as tasking, the run-time system may also support communication or initiation between distinct programs, some of which may

Run Time Implementation Considerations

not be Ada programs. Such facilities are normally provided by means of predefined packages or perhaps through features of package MACHINE_CODE.

The provision of such features may be used to support methodologies such as MASCOT and may be necessary for the operation of certain types of multiprocessor systems.

Q22.1.4 What facilities are provided by the run-time system for interaction with the environment?

The run-time system may support, by predefined packages or otherwise, interaction with the underlying hardware and operating system in ways beyond those defined by the Reference Manual. This does not imply any language extension, but rather the provision as a part of the run-time system of Ada packages (possibly with bodies in some other language) giving access to the underlying system. For example the Reference Manual does not define any mechanism for setting a real-time clock, but a package could be provided to do this. Such facilities may be at a low level as for example access to operating system storage management facilities, or higher level such as a means of accessing a database management system.

Q22.1.5 Does the run-time system support fully simultaneous operation of input-output?

Although a task calling a standard input-output procedure is always suspended until the termination of the transfer, the execution of other tasks can continue normally. An implementation where the entire program is suspended during an input-output transfer is not normally satisfactory but may be acceptable for some applications.

Q22.1.6 Are facilities provided to lock particular tasks to specific processors?

In a multiprocessor system it may be that not all processors support all facilities, for example floating-point arithmetic or direct memory access (DMA) channels, so that it may be necessary to constrain the allocation of some tasks to specific processors.

Q22.1.7 Is there dynamic allocation of tasks to processors or must allocation be done at compile time or link time?

Allocation of tasks to processors may be performed automatically by the run-time system or may have to be done explicitly by the user in advance. Automatic allocation may fix a task to a processor when the task is created or may perform dynamic reallocation of tasks to processors each time the tasks are scheduled. The strategy used and facilities provided by the run-time system may have a profound influence on the design of some real-time programs.

Where tasks are created dynamically, it is clearly necessary for some aspects of allocation to be performed at run time, but this may still be guided by a pragma or a link-time command.

Where tasks can be moved between processors then consideration of the memory configuration of the system may restrict the degree of freedom. For example, some data item to which a task requires access must be located in memory mutually shared on any processors on which the task may be required to execute.

Q22.1.8 Does the run-time system provide any support for overload protection?

Under conditions of heavy loading it may be necessary for an application to reduce its loading by modifications to its scheduling mechanisms. A run-time system may provide means to assist in such operations, for example by means of an Ada package interface, by pragmas, or by link-time commands.

Q22.1.9 How is storage for nested tasks allocated?

The storage space for a task may be allocated independently of any containing task or it may be taken from the storage of its containing task. This may have important consequences, especially if the number of tasks is not known.

Q22.1.10 Does the run-time system provide any means to prevent monopolising of resources?

It may happen that a task operating incorrectly consumes an excessive share of the processor time. To help detect this situation a run-time system might, in conjunction with a suitable pragma, provide some facility such as an interrupt when a watchdog task is not scheduled.

Q22.1.11 What are the characteristics of the exception mechanism?

The exception handling mechanism may be optimised for speed of handling an exception or for minimum overhead for unraised exceptions. This choice may also have effects at elaboration time and on the interaction with tasking, in that exceptions raised during a rendezvous may need to be treated differently.

23

Architectural Considerations

23.1 Introduction

As a language, Ada takes far greater account of computer architecture than did any other general-purpose high-level language before it. This results largely from its intended primary use in embedded computer systems and from the need to have well defined, predictable behaviour from programs irrespective of the environment in which they are used.

The embedded computer requirement contributed in two ways to the design of the language. Firstly, embedded applications inevitably involve intimate interaction with hardware, both as inputs and outputs, but also often through execution on unusual configurations of processor, storage and other computer infrastructure. Secondly, because it has been a policy of the US Department of Defense to enforce the use of Ada for programming embedded systems, the design of the language has had to incorporate as many low-level control facilities for the application system developer as were available through any earlier languages, thereby undermining many possible arguments against the use of Ada in favour of other languages.

The requirement for predictability of behaviour is not simply a requirement for portability, although it is often seen as that. In some respects it is a requirement for non-portability. That is, it is important that an application program should not appear to run in an environment for which it was specifically not designed, simply to generate erroneous results or to adopt incorrect behaviour in exceptional circumstances. The predictable behaviour in this case is that a program which takes advantage of the architectural controls provided in Ada should reject its execution environment in an appropriate way. Depending upon the exact nature of the incompatibility, this rejection could take place during execution (preferably near the start!), during the compilation process, or at some intermediate stage during the construction of the program.

Although target architecture is the only architectural consideration in an operational application, the development of an application requires account to be taken of the architectural characteristics of the host as well if they are different, as is usually the case for embedded applications. There are also factors to be considered in the mechanisms of host-target working.

104   *Architectural Considerations*

23.2   Source Code and Data Coding Issues

The Reference Manual defines the character set that is to be used for the source code of programs. It is not necessarily the case that any textual information in the application program is restricted to the same character set.

The graphical characters in the standard character set correspond to codes in the ISO seven-bit character set, ISO 646 seven-bit coded character set, and a compilation system is obliged to provide a package called ASCII which defines constants for all the characters of this code.   For an environment where ISO 646 is not the standard character set, it would be useful to have a package which defines the constants of whichever code is to be used. An example of such an alternative code is EBCDIC.

It may happen that the host and target environments have different native character sets, or that different targets employed in an application have incompatible character sets. Where two computers with different character sets are obliged to exchange textual information, particularly if that information is at some stage intended to be for human viewing, it would be useful to have some mechanism for converting between the character sets. An example of where this requirement might arise is the debugging from one host of a variety of targets.

Q23.2.1 To what extent does the compilation system support the character set of the application?

Facilities provided by a compilation system might include:

- a character type with an appropriate representation clause;

- a package of constant definitions;

- subprograms to convert between strings of the host and application character types.

Although the provision of such facilities during implementation of the application should not prove a burden, their absence, or the absence of any alternative equivalent facilities from the compilation system might be regarded a reflection on the commitment of the supplier to the target in question.

Architectural Considerations

Q23.2.2 Does the host-target debugger, if supplied, display characters and strings of the application's data in an appropriate graphical form?

The quality of any debugging aid must be judged by a number of factors, and one is the way in which it displays data values from the application being debugged. If it purports to display data in a fashion appropriate to the type of that data, then it might reasonably be expected that the display of application characters and strings would be in a form which had meaning in the context of the application. A debugging aid which does not have an awareness of character set differences has the potential for having its operation disturbed by the appearance of unanticipated characters in the application data.

Q23.2.3 How does the compilation system react when it encounters an illegal character in the source text?

The Reference Manual defines which characters are allowed in a source text. The presence of an excluded character renders a source text illegal and as such it must be rejected by a compiler. Much program preparation equipment is capable of generating illegal Ada source characters, often simply by the user pressing the Control key in combination with another key. A compilation system might handle this problem in any of a variety of ways:

- Exclude illegal characters as they arise. This technique is only feasible if Ada source text is prepared using a special purpose tool.

- Preprocess the source text. Unless the incidence of illegal characters is high, and that in itself might be a cause for concern, it is unlikely that a supplier would provide a preprocessor tool simply to filter illegal characters from source text. However, it might be that the compilation system works in conjunction with some kind of development support environment which requires source texts to be filed and registered. Preprocessing at this stage might then also be required for other reasons. It should be noted that if preprocessing is enforced for all Ada source text, the requirements for validation demand that the presence of illegal characters be reported.

- Fail the compilation. If an illegal character reaches a valid compiler, the compilation must be failed. It is unlikely in most cases that the compilation needs to be terminated before all the checking phases of the compiler have been completed.

Q23.2.4 What support does the compilation system have for national character sets?

Although the Reference Manual uses the ASCII graphical symbols, programs may be prepared using equipment which is designed for different national variants of the ISO seven-bit coded character set. A compilation system might be oblivious of this possibility, or it might be designed to provide helpful diagnostics when it detects the use of a national character in a context where the corresponding ASCII character would be illegal, for instance an accented letter in an identifier.

Q23.2.5 What restrictions does a compilation system impose on the length of a source line?

The Reference Manual does not define what range of source line lengths are acceptable for an Ada compilation system. If a compilation system imposes a maximum on the length of a source line it can process, that automatically sets an upper bound on the length of any identifier, numeric literal, or string literal that it can successfully process. Thus, if a program makes full use of the line length available with a particular compilation system, it is not possible to compile that program with a different compilation system which has a lesser maximum line length without first reformatting the program source text. Furthermore, if the program has lexical elements which make full use of the available line length, or if the second compilation system imposes other restrictions on the sizes of the lexical elements, it is necessary to rewrite the program before it can be recompiled with the second compilation system.

A compilation system might reasonably be expected to accept source lines which are at least compatible in length with the width offered by commonly used program preparation equipment. Text indentation is likely to place demands on the full width available with such equipment.

It is open to a compilation system to impose different length limitations according, for example, to the contents of a line. This would allow a compilation system to accept as valid Ada, source text which has Ada comments extending beyond its nominal line length limitations.

The particular requirements in this respect should be assessed by the application system developer, taking into account any existing source text which would need to be compiled.

Q23.2.6 What restrictions does a compilation system impose on the length of an identifier?

All characters of an identifier are significant and the Reference Manual does not introduce any length constraint. An upper bound is set by any line length restrictions imposed by a compilation system, but it is

Architectural Considerations

conceivable that a more severe restriction is imposed, particularly if very long lines are accepted. It is not possible to offer any guidelines as to what is a reasonable restriction, and therefore the particular requirements of the application, taking into account any existing source code that is to be compiled, should first be assessed.

It should be considered that the use of long identifiers may result in increased restrictions on the number of identifiers allowed by a compilation system, and this is an aspect which should also be investigated.

Q23.2.7 What restrictions does a compilation system impose on the length of a numeric literal?

The Reference Manual does not specify any length constraints on a numeric literal. An upper bound is set by any line length restriction, but in practice, it is likely that a much severer restriction could be tolerated. The acceptability of any restrictions needs to be considered in relation to the predefined types of the target. For example, it might be a requirement to write a binary based literal corresponding to the largest predefined integer type, excluding universal integer. The number of significant digits allowed in a real literal might be expected to provide sufficient accuracy for expressing literal values for the predefined floating point type which has the greatest floating accuracy definition, and for expressing literal values of the predefined fixed point type with the largest mantissa.

If restrictions are imposed on the length of numeric literals, it would be appropriate to investigate whether these restrictions are affected by the presence of leading or trailing zeros, and whether there are ways to circumvent these restrictions, such as by using an alternative notation.

Q23.2.8 What restrictions does a compilation system impose on the length of a string literal?

Q23.2.9 What restrictions does a compilation system impose on the lexical length of a string literal?

It is necessary to distinguish the lexical length in this instance since the Reference Manual defines the length of a string literal to be the number of character values in the sequence represented, that is excluding the string brackets and counting each doubled quotation character within the literal as a single character.

The Reference Manual does not specify any length constraints for a string literal, although any constraints a compilation system imposes on the length of a line presents an upper bound. In practice, since the language provides the means to concatenate string literals, it is in principle possible to construct a sequence of character values which is as long as may be required. However, if an implementation does impose restrictions on the length of a string literal, the restriction needs to be considered in relation to any existing Ada source code that is to be compiled.

Concatenation of literals notwithstanding, it is conceivable that there is a limitation imposed by the target on the length of a sequence of character values which itself imposes an upper bound on the length of a string literal.

23.3 Ability to Change Host

Despite the standardisation of Ada, each compilation system is different, having its own strengths and weaknesses, its own set of tools, and its own methods of working. It is now rare that an Ada compilation system is to be bought for use in the implementation of just one application. A purchaser more usually has the expectation that Ada will be used for some time into the future. Although it is to be anticipated that the user expects to build up expertise in the use of one principal host computer, it is to be expected that over the lifetime of the Ada language, there will be considerable evolution in the development of hardware, leading the application system developer to the purchase of further hosts for which Ada support will be needed. Additionally, many Ada applications will have a lifetime in excess of that of the host computer on which the application code was compiled. Therefore, again, there is a need to see Ada support continuing across a sequence of different host computers.

In both these examples there is the need to continue with the same Ada compilation system as far as possible. In the first case the need is to preserve expertise and to avoid disruptive changes in methods of working. In the second case it is the basic need to provide an evolutionary maintenance path without the need to replace the whole application when the host is replaced.

Q23.3.1 Is the same (or a variant) compilation system available on other host computers?

It can never be possible to guarantee that an Ada compilation system will remain compatible in every respect, let alone across a change in hosts. Nevertheless, attention to the portability aspect by the supplier might be regarded as a favourable indication: a compilation system which was never designed to be portable is unlikely to achieve a performance on a new host which is comparable with that on its original host without considerable effort.

Fortunately, economics dictate that a compilation system supplier must attempt to supply systems for a variety of machines unless the supplier also markets a particular host. Therefore many compilation systems available

Architectural Considerations

have already had their portability demonstrated. Even systems which appear to be proprietary to a particular hardware supplier often have their origins in more widely available systems.

Q23.3.2 Was the compilation system designed for a particular architectural class of host computer?

Q23.3.3 On which different kinds of host is the compilation system supported?

Even a demonstrably portable compilation system may have its limitations. For example, it may be restricted in respect of certain architectural features: it may be unable to accommodate more than a limited address range, or it may be unable to perform arithmetic on numbers greater than some historically arbitrary maximum. As hardware develops, the tendency is to remove restrictions which the compilation system was designed either to get round or to operate within. Therefore a portable system may be unable to take full advantage of new hardware and so function less efficiently.

Q23.3.4 Does the supplier permit other organisations to rehost the compilation system?

Q23.3.5 Has any other organisation successfully rehosted the compilation system?

Q23.3.6 Has any other organisation attempted and failed to rehost the compilation system?

Q23.3.7 What support does the supplier provide to organisations wishing to rehost the compilation system?

There is a limit to the number of different hosts that the average supplier is likely to be prepared to support. It may be open to the application system developer who has specific requirements to commission the transfer of the compilation system to a chosen host. The actual transfer might be performed by the supplier, the intending application system developer, or some third party. If the application system developer or a third party is to undertake the work, this is practical only if the supplier has taken appropriate steps to make available, not only source or code libraries, but adequate documentation and consultancy advice.

23.4 Range of Targets Supported

Micro-electronics is a rapidly developing field, developing so rapidly in fact that an application designed for an existing processor often appears obsolete when viewed in the light of announcements from the hardware suppliers.

The implementation of an Ada compilation system is a major undertaking. Development of new compilation systems is unlikely to keep pace with hardware developments if a new product has to be developed from scratch for each new processor.

It is seldom the case that a user of Ada is developing a single application. More usually, there are:

- variants of an application using different processors according to performance requirements;

- applications which use different processors to perform a collection of different functions;

- a service life which requires upgrades to new processors as they become available;

- and of course a variety of applications in related fields across the application system developer's business.

These circumstances combine to suggest that, in selecting a compilation system, more than just the current target processor should be considered. It may be pertinent to consider other processors in the same range, as well as competing processors. The extent to which a supplier already covers the field may give some indication of the potential the compilation system has for adaption to future target processors.

Q23.4.1 What are the targets currently supported by the compilation system?

Q23.4.2 What other targets does the supplier plan to offer?

It may be that the supplier has no plans to support a target which is of particular interest to the application system developer. This is likely to be the case where the target of interest has a limited field of application or is special in some other way. This problem can still be overcome if the compilation system has been designed with adaption for different targets in mind, in which case there may be various routes to acquiring the required system.

Architectural Considerations

Q23.4.3 Does the supplier operate a service for adapting the compilation system to different targets?

If the supplier operates an adaption service, it may be that, once the system has been adapted to the new target, the supplier is prepared to market and support it as a product, thus helping to defray the cost of adaption.

Q23.4.4 Does the supplier make available and support a product which enables the compilation system to be adapted to other targets?

Q23.4.5 Is there a body of expertise able to use such an adaption product, either within the application system developer's organisation or elsewhere?

Adaption of the compilation system by a third party or in house should be evaluated in the context of continuing support and maintenance of the product.

Q23.4.6 Does the compilation system impose constraints which are not inherent in the target?

Although the existence of support for a range of targets may satisfy the basic requirement, it is not necessarily the case that all such targets are equally well supported. Different processors may have different architectures. Unless the design of the compilation system is sufficiently flexible, it may not be possible to generate code which takes full advantage of a particular target architecture. Alternatively, a rough and ready approach may have been taken to cover the widest range of processors with the minimum of effort. For example, a compilation system which assumes a stack architecture may generate code which fails to make use of all the registers that a target has available. Even where a coherent range of targets is supported, it may be that the compilation system does not take account of all the facilities of the more powerful processors in the range. For example, it may impose size constraints on an application which are only applicable to the less powerful processors.

Constraints may be imposed which are of no relevance to the applications considered. Therefore it is important to review any constraints with the intended applications in mind. For example, a size constraint may be imposed which is already above the needs of the application.

Q23.4.7 Are there features of the target of which the compilation system makes little or no use?

Again it is important to consider the significance of any such features to the intended applications. The nature of the Ada language may actually make the use of some features inefficient or inappropriate, for example a table translate instruction or vector instructions. Therefore the justification for any non-use of features must be evaluated carefully.

Conversely, the need to meet the requirements of the language, possibly in a way which is compatible across a range of targets, may have led to an inappropriate use of facilities on some targets. An example of this might be the support for a wide addressing range on a target for which the machine instructions have a limited addressing range resulting in a large overhead on some or all address manipulations. The effect of such an approach could result in any array accesses being very inefficient.

Another example of a potential mismatch between the target facilities and the language implementation is the use of the processor stack. The processor may provide instructions which support stack growth in one direction whereas the compiled code may be structured for a stack which grows the other way, again using inefficient code sequences to achieve the required effect.

Q23.4.8 Are there any features of Ada, or facilities provided, which make use of the target in ways which, in other circumstances, might not be considered sensible?

Clearly this is not a question that is easily answered. There will often be quirks which are difficult to eliminate and which are so rare or so minor as not to have any significant impact on an application. What is sought is any known problem that a supplier would find embarrassing if he had failed to make an intending purchaser aware of it.

Q23.4.9 Are there rules or guidelines for an application system developer to avoid use of inefficient target code sequences?

A good compilation system supplier should ensure customer satisfaction by making such advice available, so that it can be heeded when performance is critical.

Q23.4.10 To what extent does the compilation system achieve compatibility across a range of processors?

Q23.4.11 What sacrifices or compromises have been made to achieve range compatibility?

An application system developer should consider the extent to which range compatibility is required and the extent to which the application can be adapted to take account of any differences in the characteristics of the compilation system across the range.

23.5 Support for Multiprocessor Target

Although Ada as a language provides facilities to define the parallel execution of tasks, it does not offer any mechanism for mapping such tasks on to different processors of a multiprocessor target configuration. Neither does the language itself take account of any addressing restrictions that might be imposed by the target architecture, such as the inaccessibility of certain areas of store to some of the processors.

Recent developments in hardware have resulted in providing the engineer with the components to construct a wide variety of different configurations of processors, stores and busses, with the net effect that there is no obvious standard for the software supplier to address. By the same token, there is no simple set of questions that the application system developer of a compilation system should address in this context, since requirements are likely to be considerably revised as different hardware approaches are adopted. Therefore, it is particularly important in this area that the compilation system is viewed with a clear understanding of the current requirements and future trends for the application target hardware.

Q23.5.1 Has the supplier provided a compilation system for any other multiprocessor architecture?

Q23.5.2 Has the supplier been involved in the provision of software for a multiprocessor application?

Multiprocessor applications are generally significantly different from single processor applications in a number of respects. Unless a supplier has experience of the kinds of problems that can arise in practice, it is possible that limitations in the compilation system may not be recognised soon enough. Depending upon the architecture and the precise requirements, a number of different features may be relevant.

Q23.5.3 Does the system enable the application system developer to specify where a particular part of the application is to be located?

Q23.5.4 Can the location of both code and data be controlled by the user?

Q23.5.5 What is the granularity of location? For example, is the unit of location a package, a subprogram, an individual data item, or some other unit? Is location specified by an absolute address, defining an area, or by some other means?

Q23.5.6 Can units be aggregated for collocation?

From the answers to these questions a measure can be obtained of how much flexibility the compilation system provides for mapping the application program into the available stores of the target. A further question is associated with these.

Q23.5.7 At what stage is the storage mapping specified?

If it is necessary for the application developer to specify the location of a unit as part of the source code (for example by a pragma or an address clause) then if any need arises to relocate the unit, a recompilation is required. Also, this solution necessitates having different versions of the source if the same unit is to be located differently in different variant releases of the application. A compilation system may provide for location specification as part of the linking process. This might also provide the means for collocating a collection of units. Although this avoids the recompilation overhead, it does not necessarily remove the configuration management problem of having variant linked units for different configurations.

A further possibility is for location to be specified as part of the target loading process. This gives considerable flexibility at the expense of complex steering files for the loader. There may also be overheads if links have to be established as part of the initialisation of the application program.

Q23.5.8 What mechanisms are provided for calling common code from multiple processors?

The preceding discussion has concerned itself with the static allocation of units of the software. There may also be a dynamic aspect to consider. For example, it may be required to call the same subprogram from tasks running on different processors which have no program store in common.

It might be that a compilation system only provides this facility where the code can be loaded into store which is in the address space of all the processors which want to call it. Alternatively, it might duplicate the code as required. A further possibility is that the run-time system might

Architectural Considerations

implement a remote procedure call so the code is actually executed on an appropriate processor. The relative efficiency of these different solutions depends to some extent on the available tasks for the different processors and the degree of coupling between the processors.

Q23.5.9 What facilities are there to control which processor is used to execute a task?

Q23.5.10 Is execution of a task confined to a particular processor or is it dynamic in some way?

Just as code and data need to be located, so also do tasks. Tasks can also be static or dynamic.

If a task is statically declared, it might be possible to specify on which processor it is to be executed in much the same way as it was suggested earlier that code and data could be located. Such a facility places the onus on the application system developer to resolve questions of system utilisation. If the run-time system is able to transfer the execution of a task between different processors to take advantage of available resources, a measure of control is required when not all processors have access to the same facilities.

Q23.5.11 How are storage and processors allocated to dynamically activated tasks?

Ada allows for multiple copies of dynamic tasks to be initiated at any time during the execution of the program, but provides no mechanism for specifying where the dynamic data for such a task is to be located or which processor is to be used for its execution.

The factors here may depend on where the code is located and the current context of the program. The same considerations of control of system utilisation apply as for static tasks.

Q23.5.12 What facilities does the compilation system have to assist with mapping the application program to the target configuration and for detecting potentially unworkable mappings?

The Ada language does not consider the possibility that there may be access restrictions on code and data other than those imposed by the visibility and scoping rules of the language. Some additional aid is required by the application system developer to detect and avoid restrictions imposed by the target.

Any tools provided in this area will obviously depend on what facilities the compilation system provides for control. Probably the most useful facilities are those which can be applied from the design stage since the primary issue is one of design. But it is also necessary to police the actual implementation so that any attempt by the application developer to produce code which would contravene the architectural constraints can be quickly detected and rectified.

As an alternative to preventing the construction of malformed systems, the compilation system might provide a sophisticated run time kernel which has the capability of hiding the target structure. Such a kernel would relieve the designer of the need to accommodate the restrictions in the target architecture at the expense of potential overheads during execution. Thus care would be needed to ensure that the benefits and overheads are properly assessed.

23.6 The Target Environment

The Ada language was designed for use in embedded computer applications. At the time the language was specified, it was unusual for an embedded computer to have an operating system of any kind. The term "operating system" carried with it connotations of excessive consumption of both processing power and space, neither of which were copiously available on the microprocessors of the time. Therefore Ada was designed so that all the housekeeping facilities that an embedded application might require could be incorporated in the program itself by the compilation system.

The objectives notwithstanding, early implementations of Ada compilation systems chose computers with operating systems for their targets. In the time it has taken for compilation systems to develop to the state when they can be used to address bare target processors, the microprocessors have themselves developed in power, capacity and complexity to the extent that the presence of an operating system is no longer seen as such a penalty, and may even be an essential ingredient to the efficient development of an application.

The same period has also seen the development of what are termed real-time operating systems. These are small, efficient kernels which include no more facilities than are strictly essential for utility use in embedded applications. Typically they provide support for asynchronous or pseudo-asynchronous tasks, including inter-task communication, synchronisation and scheduling, together with basic input-output control. They are configurable so that only the components an application requires need to be included, and routines specific to the application can be substituted.

Architectural Considerations

Q23.6.1 Under which regimes does the target addressed by the compilation system run?

An Ada compilation system may be designed to provide code for a target running in any of these regimes:

- under a comprehensive operating system;

- in conjunction with a real-time operating system;

- as a bare target.

Each regime has its strengths and weaknesses, and which is best for a particular application can only be determined when a large number of factors have been considered. Although it may be relatively easy to distinguish between extremes, this Guide can only point the reader in the right direction.

Q23.6.2 How much store is taken up by the operating system or other run-time support software, and how much is available to an application program?

Q23.6.3 What percentage of the processing power of the target is available to application programs?

Even a bare target has a run-time system supplied by the compilation system to provide housekeeping services.

Q23.6.4 What effect does any operating system have on the real-time response of the program?

An operating system may introduce delays between the detection of an external stimulus and its presentation to an application program. It may also impose scheduling constraints which have the effect, among others, of extending the periods requested in delay statements.

Q23.6.5 What is the effect on program execution of the initiation of an input or output operation?

Operating systems frequently control the execution of input and output operations. Because of the need to protect data during block transfers, they often inhibit program execution while a transfer is in progress. There may be degrees of sophistication which restrict this inhibition to, for example, only the task requesting the transfer.

118   *Architectural Considerations*

Q23.6.6 What scope is there for the incorporation of specialised device drivers?

Q23.6.7 Are there templates for device drivers which can be customised for a particular application?

An embedded application may have little call for standard input and output services. Often it involves access to custom-made devices which the application developer has built and which require specialised drivers.

23.6.8 What facilities are provided for intelligent interaction with the target during application development and testing?

Absence of operating system facilities from a target may limit the scope for program development on the target. For example, there may be no filing system; if there is any form of operator console at all, debug interaction may be restricted to interrogation by absolute address. In these circumstances, there may be some linkage provided to a host or other intelligent device whereby operator interaction with an application in development can be achieved.

Q23.6.9 Does program development or program loading require the presence of a monitor routine on the target?

Q23.6.10 What constraints are there on the location of any monitor in the target?

Q23.6.11 Is sufficient information supplied for an application designer to provide an alternative monitor routine?

Q23.6.12 Can the compilation system be adapted to use a different monitor?

One mechanism for interaction with a bare target requires the presence of a monitor routine on the target. This routine plays no part in the normal operation of the target, but is only used during testing. It may also be used during program loading, and therefore may be supplied as a ROM. Whether it is held in ROM or RAM it takes up some part of the program's address space, and therefore cannot be entirely ignored, although during normal operation of the program it may be overwritten or hidden.

23.7   Run-time Modification

System reliability was one of the objectives of the design of the Ada language. It is generally believed that reliability can be achieved by

Architectural Considerations

thorough specification of the requirements followed by a design and an implementation in which careful checks are made that each stage is entirely compatible with the earlier stage. Ada assists in this process by ensuring that all components in an assembled piece of software are mutually compatible, at least as far as their Ada interdependences are concerned.

Q23.7.1 What facilities are provided to minimise the time and effort required to make a change to an operational system?

When it is necessary to make changes in a system constructed like this, perhaps because of a change in requirements, each step must be reworked, at least as far as it is dependent on the change, and again the Ada compilation system will ensure that appropriate source code is recompiled together with dependent code, and the system rebuilt. The price for such a degree of reliability may be a significant amount of time and effort, depending upon the size of the system, but not necessarily on the extent of the basic change.

In practice, although high reliability may be important, there may be other ways of achieving it, and there may be other factors which are even more important, such as continuity of service. Therefore, where there is an application for which it is not acceptable to impose long development delays while a change is incorporated, it is pertinent to seek a compilation system which provides alternative methods for developing and incorporating changes. Methods might range from sophisticated optimisations in the compilation process to blatant emergency patching. It should be noted that mechanisms of the latter kind invalidate the application system's acceptance testing, and therefore they need to be accompanied by other mechanisms which help to ensure that any change so incorporated is reintroduced into the authorised software.

Q23.7.2 If an unchecked mechanism is provided for making emergency changes to an operational system, what facilities are provided for ensuring that an equivalent change is also applied to the authorised source and is subsequently approved?

Compilation system optimisations might be used to avoid unnecessary recompilations. An assertion mechanism might be provided to allow the user to assert that certain recompilations were unnecessary, although this is a case where it would be necessary to have the assertions checked before the authorised version of the program library is updated.

Q23.7.3 What facilities are provided for minimising the time and effort required to change between versions of an operational program?

Where it is important that a system remain in operation across changes, various possibilities might be offered, which may or may not have implications for the actual application design. A fast changeover between two co-resident versions may be one solution. Variants of this scheme might allow changeover of individual parts of the system, and this may be particularly appropriate where the application is distributed across a number of processing modules.

Q23.7.4 What facilities are provided for dynamic reconfiguration of an operational system, either manually or automatically?

Apart from changes to the actual code of an operational program, there may be a requirement that the program take account of changes in its environment. Such changes generally are a matter for consideration by the run-time system rather than the application itself, and may be required to cope with component failures and restoration of service. Thus a system may be required to cope with variations in the amount of storage and the number of processors available.

23.8 Code and Data Sharing

Many target systems have the power to support multiple, simultaneous applications. In such an environment, if machine code which is common to more than one application can be shared, there may be considerable savings in the storage requirements for the processor, often an important factor in embedded computer applications. Shareable components may be standard libraries, which may have been pre-compiled, or libraries created by the user.

Q23.8.1 Can the Ada compilation system be used to prepare libraries of software or other support software which can be shared simultaneously by multiple Ada application programs?

The Ada language does not lend itself naturally for use as the source code for shared libraries for various technical reasons such as the absence of a main program and the determination of an order for elaboration. To make the compilation system suitable for the compilation of shared libraries, the supplier may have provided additional facilities or tools, or specified particular techniques. For example, there may be tools for installing such a library, and initialisation and termination subprograms to be called by users of the library.

Architectural Considerations

Q23.8.2 Can a program be linked and loaded to interface to resident code which is shared by other co-resident programs?

Major parts of run-time support software and operating systems may be written in Ada, and despite the comments above, Ada may also be used for writing libraries of software. Where multiple application programs are running simultaneously in the same processor, it is useful if such libraries, as well as run time support software, can be made available to all the application programs without the need for code duplication. How code is shared is a function of the architecture, the compilation processes used to compile both the shared code and the code which is sharing it, and the program linking and loading processes.

Q23.8.3 To what extent are shared library routines integrated with an application program, and what constraints do their use impose on application programs?

The degree to which sharing can take place may vary between systems. For example, a shared library may become more or less integral with an application program, providing type declarations, subprogram calls and exceptions; or it may provide a tasking interface; or it may exist effectively as a separate program with some form of message exchange with application programs. Each of these solutions may affect the style of programming required to use the shared code effectively.

Q23.8.4 Does the compilation system provide any mechanism whereby all or any part of the run-time support software may be shared between multiple application programs running concurrently?

An important library of software which is a candidate for being shared is the Ada run-time support software.

The Ada run-time support software can occupy many kilobytes of storage. If the Ada run-time support software is replicated across all the application programs, then proportionately more store is occupied by what are generally identical copies of the same code. Alternative approaches which may be adopted by compilation system suppliers separate the run-time support software from the application software in much the same way as an operating system would be separated. Thus, the run-time support software may be shared between multiple application programs in just the same way as an operating system would be shared.

Q23.8.5 What interfaces to the run-time support software are defined and usable explicitly by application programs?

The compilation system supplier may make the run-time support software accessible through defined interfaces. Normally these interfaces would be used automatically by the compiled code, but there may be some which, in certain circumstances, may be usefully called explicitly from an application program. An example of the use of such a facility is to initiate garbage collection during a period of low activity in the application.

Q23.8.6 What parts of the run-time support software may be replaced and what guidance is provided for this replacement?

A further advantage of defined interfaces to the run-time support software is that they may enable the user of the compilation system to replace all or part of the standard support software supplied by alternative routines which may be better attuned to the intended application, or which may form part of a resident operating system or real time executive. It should be noted that replacement of the run-time support software may have an impact on the validation status of the compilation system.

Q23.8.7 What facilities does the compilation system provide for data to be shared between co-resident application programs?

Just as there may be libraries of shared code, there may also be regions of shareable data. Typically such regions would be used to contain large tables of constants, but could conceivably be used to contain dynamic data from a data collection system, or where particularly loose coupling between programs was required.

Q23.8.8 What locking mechanisms are available should it be required to protect data which is shared between co-resident programs?

Where more than one program is allowed to update data in a shared region, it is usually necessary to have a mechanism which ensures that only one such program has access to the region, or some defined part of it, at any one time. This is required in order to provide data consistency. It should be possible to guarantee that there are no corruptions resulting from simultaneous attempts to update the same group of items, and that no program can read from such a group of items until the program updating them has completed that activity. Additionally it may be required that some of the programs accessing a shared region can only read it whereas other programs have write access as well.

Architectural Considerations

Although it is usually possible for the user to implement some such mechanism, where the compilation system permits direct addressing of storage, a compilation system which provides more sophisticated techniques for data sharing may also provide mechanisms for controlling access to shared data as part of its run-time software.

Q23.8.9 Can shared libraries be used by programs compiled with a different compilation system from that used to compile the shared library?

Q23.8.10 Can shared libraries be used by programs written in a different language?

It is usual for support software, such as libraries, to be written in accordance with an interface specification. Provided application programs conform to this interface specification, no constraints are placed on how the application programs are generated. Programs may be written in different languages or may be compiled by different compilation systems. However, as was observed above, there may have to be additional software or subprogram calls associated with the use of the library.

23.9 Host-Target Development

It is common practice to develop programs for an embedded target on a more sophisticated host computer. Whilst the target may have very limited program development facilities, no native compiler and a decidedly unfriendly user interface, a host may offer everything that a programmer could consider necessary for the orderly development of software. The technique then becomes to develop the software as far as possible on the host, and only transfer development to the target when that is the only efficient way to complete the task.

There are several phases through which a development of this kind might pass:

- Generate the program for execution on the host in native mode and test all those functions which are not specific to the target.

- Generate the program as for the target but execute it through a target simulator on the host to test those functions which are specific to the target but which do not rely on real-time execution or live data.

- Transfer the program to the target and test it through some linkage to the host.

Architectural Considerations

Q23.9.1 Are there compatible compilers on the host, (that is, a native compiler for compiling code for execution on the host, and a cross-compiler for compiling code for execution on the target)?

Despite the standardisation of the language and validation of compilers, it is still possible to discover incompatibilities between compilers. For example, there may be differences in the pragmas that are accepted, in the representation specifications that are supported, and even in the sizes for the predefined types. Compatibility in the accompanying tool set is also very useful.

Q23.9.2 Is there a target simulator on the host?

The value of a target simulator is likely to depend on just how difficult it is to debug the target directly. For example, there may be no adequate human interface on the target, or more severe still, the target hardware may not have reached a usable state of development at the time software testing is to begin. Conversely, a simplistic simulator may give a false impression of how the program will behave on the target.

Q23.9.3 What mechanisms are there for transferring programs from the host to the target?

Factors to be considered are the time taken to transfer programs of the size envisaged, and the reliability of the medium and protocols. The ability to transfer only parts of programs may also be useful. Common transfer mechanisms include an asynchronous link with a checksum, a local area network, and probes into the target bus structure.

Q23.9.4 To what extent can target execution be controlled and monitored from the host?

When the program is being executed on the target, only a subset of the debugging facilities that were available on the host may still be available. Conversely, there may be extended debugging features for probing the run time support software.

Q23.9.5 What is the extent of the disruption to normal execution of the program on the target when debugging is performed through the host?

Disruption may take the form of a resident monitor on the target for host-to-target communication which itself may perform a relatively passive role. Nevertheless, the fact that there is communication between the host and the target which is not a component activity of an operational system reduces the validity of any attempts to assess the real-time performance of the application software. Timing problems in the operational system may be hidden whilst irrelevant problems may be introduced. Alternatively, the host may execute its control through probes into the various logic, data and address lines of the target with no apparent effect on normal operation.

Q23.9.6 How may a program running in a target processor be debugged once the target processor is disconnected from the host?

The ability to debug a program in an embedded target is likely to be very target dependent. There are on the market various electronic devices which can be used to probe the logic, data and address lines of the target, some capable of being primed by the host and sufficiently sophisticated to be regarded as not much different from hosts themselves in this context. Other mechanisms may rely on the continued presence of a monitor and a suitable port to support a terminal which may then be used to debug the program in terms of machine addresses and bit patterns.

There are further questions and discussions relating to these topics in chapter 19, Compilation System Facilities.

24

Man-Machine Interface

24.1 Introduction

The quality of the man-machine interface to an Ada compilation system significantly affects the user's ability to use the compilation system effectively. It is of little benefit for a compilation system to have extensive facilities if they are very difficult to use.

A factor to consider when assessing a man-machine interface is the experience of the users involved. Compilation systems may provide a very suitable interface for an inexperienced user, but once that user has spent time with the system the help it provides may become cumbersome and costly in time. A different difficulty could be that the system provides complex facilities that are easy to call up, but it requires experience to interpret the results in a meaningful way. When the results from complex facilities are made so readily available an inexperienced user could obtain them and then use them incorrectly with unfortunate consequences.

It can therefore be seen that when assessing a man-machine interface there are many different factors which must be taken into account, for example the skills and learning ability of the users and the length of time the system will be used for. The following questions give an indication of the different attributes a man-machine interface may be required to have, but they are not applicable in all project environments.

24.2 The Development Environment

This is the prime area for interaction between the user and the Ada compilation system. The experience of the development team directly affects the requirements on the interface and method of working. An experienced team may be available to assist in the resolution of any problems, above a specified complexity, that a development team may find. Alternatively each development team may need to solve its own problems so that experience becomes more uniform within the team and between teams.

Q24.2.1 What form does the user interface take?

There are many different styles that the user interface can take and it is mainly a matter of project preference when deciding if the style is suitable. The possible styles include command language, menus and icons. If the

Ada compilation system is one tool in a set of tools to be used by the project, uniformity of styles across the whole set is appropriate, even though there may be differences of detail between the tools. For example, all the tools may use menus, but not necessarily in exactly the same form.

It may also be possible to tailor the style for the project because different options are provided by the compilation system. The experience of the project team again influences the preferred style. Within a style there are differences of usage known as "look and feel", for instance the exact actions needed to select from a menu with a mouse, or the effect of control and escape keys. Although less difficult to cope with than gross differences of style, uniformity of look and feel across a set of tools is a considerable benefit, especially to an inexperienced team.

Q24.2.2 How easy is the compilation system to use?

This is a very difficult matter to assess because it is greatly dependent on the experience of the application development team and the project application. The different aspects of the system which should be considered are:

- whether tools need to be individually invoked or are sequentially invoked by a co-ordinating tool;

- what compiling and system building options and parameters are available;

- the use of the compilation system in batch mode as well as interactive mode, for example for long overnight jobs;

- providing parameter values and initiating the application program.

Q24.2.3 How is the informational output expressed?

This concerns the error reporting from the compiler and maps generated by the linker. The requirements for the style and quantity of error messages varies considerably depending on the experience of users. Some compilation systems offer the opportunity to select the level of messages required so that all users can receive error messages that are appropriate to them. Other systems provide references to sections of the Reference Manual for further information, if that is required by the user. It should be noted if the latter system is used that the Reference Manual can be particularly difficult to read in certain sections.

Apart from the importance of the content of the error message its presentation should also be considered. Some compilation systems embed the message in the text after the line in error; in this case the way the error is marked needs to be clear so that it is not overlooked. Other compilation systems give all the error messages at the end of the text and provide references back to the lines in error; here the type of reference system used can obviously effect how quickly the error can be correctly identified and solved.

It may be necessary to examine the linkage maps generated by the linker in order to locate where variables and other entities are stored. A linkage map can be very intimidating to an inexperienced user who nevertheless needs to obtain the information.

If the users of the system are all novices to Ada compilation systems, for example if it is to be exclusively used by trainees, then assessment of these aspects is relatively simple. However if the system needs to be used as the users gain more and more experience then there could also be a requirement to be able to select the level of information presented.

Q24.2.4 What is the style of the editor?

The facilities of the editor are described in chapter 19, Compilation System Facilities but they are closely linked with the style of the editor. Many editors currently available are screen based and operate in a similar way to a word processor. The control of the editor can be by commands, function keys, menus or icons in a similar way to the general user interface of the Ada compilation system. It is unlikely that a choice is given within a single editor but the compilation system may offer the ability to use a number of editors.

Apart from the general operation of the editor there may also be variations in the levels of support it gives, for example syntax driven so that specific operations can allow the user to supply the variable parts of a particular structure and the editor provides the standard parts. The way this can be used and its flexibility are features of the style of the editor.

Q24.2.5 What form does the debugger take?

The facilities of the debugger are described in chapter 19, Compilation System Facilities however the operation of the debugger is also important. The ability to append debug commands together to form a sequence can be very useful when testing software. How the debug commands are specified, that is the debug language, can greatly influence its ease of use. The debugger is mainly used at times when the user is trying to determine why the software is not performing as expected, or to demonstrate that the software is performing as expected. It is therefore necessary for its use to be easy and very adaptable so that it can provide beneficial help rather than add uncertainty that a result may be attributable to misuse of the debugger.

Q24.2.6 What form does the target loader take?

The facilities of the target loader are described in chapter 19, Compilation System Facilities but the way it is used can also be very important. Frequently a target loader is used when the software is to be executed on a bare machine which has few facilities of its own. When this is the situation the target loader may be very complex as it compensates for this lack of facilities. The ease with which it can be used has greater importance because it may be very difficult to confirm that the software has been loaded as intended and that errors seen are not caused by incorrect loading, for example by giving a wrong address.

Q24.2.7 Can the documenting facilities be amended or extended?

The compilation system may provide facilities to pretty-print or reformat the Ada source text. The ability to describe easily the form any output is to take improves the usage of the system and enables project-specific standards to be enforced.

Q24.2.8 How accessible is the compilation system?

The accessibility of the system can be considered as an integrity issue because if access is too easy then it may be that objects in the compilation system are inadvertently altered or, worse, deleted. Alternatively if the access is difficult then it acts as a barrier to inexperienced authorised users who can quickly become disillusioned. It must be noted that unauthorised access, particularly to the program library must be prevented.

Q24.2.9 How is the access to the compilation system controlled?

The security of the compilation system can be controlled by the use of passwords, for example, so that unauthorised access, particularly to the program library, is prevented. An elaborate hierarchy of passwords could be used to provide different security levels for users cleared to different security classifications. There may alternatively be security mechanisms involving hardware, for example dongles, which must be in place on the processor before the compilation system can be invoked. This mechanism can also be used to control the use of unauthorised copies of the compilation system.

25

Language-Related Characteristics

25.1 Use of Machine Code

Although Ada goes further than most high-level languages in catering for the kind of machine-specific situations where previously the only recourse would have been the use of machine code, there are still situations where machine code is required. Machine code may be employed where size or speed is critical and available compilers have not yet reached the quality required. It may also be used where tried and trusted machine code routines already exist for a particular function. Further examples of the need to use machine code arise where there is a requirement to interface to a hardware device or a software system that is not provided for by the compiler available. This can happen where the target machine has special instructions for controlling the device, or the device uses special data formats, such as floating point values which are packed differently from the form the target normally uses. There may also be complex instructions written in microcode by the user, and the only way to use these instructions is directly through the use of machine code.

Q25.1.1 Is the use of machine-code supported, and if so how?

There are various ways in which this can be done. One is the provision of a predefined package MACHINE_CODE; this allows a machine-code subprogram to be written as a sequence of special record aggregates, one per instruction. This is adequate for short sequences but is not likely to offer the convenience of a good assembler if there is much machine code required, and of course does not help with existing code. In these cases it may be possible to use pragma INTERFACE to incorporate assembly language routines into an Ada program.

Detailed aspects of the machine-code facilities that may well be of interest include the following:

- whether entities in the Ada source program can be referred to from the machine code;

- whether pragma INLINE is available for machine-code subprograms;

- whether the use of machine-code subprograms interferes with debugging;

- whether all machine code instructions and addressing modes are available;

- if pragma INTERFACE to assembly code is provided, whether it generates special code to match calling conventions in the assembly language, or whether the assembly language subprograms must accommodate the Ada calling conventions, and in the latter case whether the information required is available.

25.2 Interfacing to Other Languages

There is less reason to want to mix Ada with other high-level languages than with machine-code, but there still may be occasions when it is required: pre-existing code, or special languages for special purposes. The mechanism here is pragma INTERFACE.

Q25.2.1 Is pragma INTERFACE provided for other high-level languages and what is the extent of the facilities it provides?

Particular aspects of pragma INTERFACE which may well be of interest include:

- which languages can be called;

- which specific compilers must be used for compiling those languages;

- any restrictions that may be imposed on the types and modes of parameters and returned values that can be passed through the interface;

- the extent to which the compilation system protects the user against dubious use of the interface by, for example, issuing warnings if an attempt is made to pass a parameter of an inappropriate type.

A two-dimensional array passed to a Fortran subroutine might be considered as a dubious use due to the different ways in which Ada and Fortran arrays are organised.

Q25.2.2 Can Ada subprograms be called from code written in other languages and if so, how comprehensive is the facility?

Before a piece of Ada code can be executed, it is necessary to have an appropriate run-time code environment in existence to provide such facilities as store management, exception trapping and task control. Such a code environment is set up at the start of execution of an Ada program, and so the facility might be provided using a program invocation mechanism, either in the other language or in the operating system. Program invocation

Language-Related Characteristics

for each call of a piece of Ada code has the effect that data can only be retained across calls if it is preserved in files, and therefore the creation of a fresh code environment on each call may not be acceptable. Retention of the code environment between calls might be achieved through an interleaved system with Ada code at a higher level setting up its code environment and then calling code compiled from the alternative language. This latter code would then, whilst preserving the Ada code environment, make calls on the Ada code at a lower level.

It is conceivable that an integrated system might adopt a run-time code environment which is compatible across Ada and other selected languages, thus facilitating mutual calls.

25.3 Unsafe Programming

Unsafe programming refers to two facilities supported by predefined generic units: unchecked deallocation to release storage space at any time, and unchecked conversion to treat a value of one type as though it were of another. They are unsafe in that their use cuts across the checks imposed by the compiler and can lead to programs running wild; nonetheless there are occasions when they are needed and the compiler must support them to some extent. The questions are as follows.

Q25.3.1 To what extent is unsafe programming supported?

Compilation systems may restrict, for example, the types to which unchecked conversion may be applied.

Q25.3.2 For unchecked deallocation, is the storage space nominally released by use of this facility actually freed for subsequent use?

If unchecked deallocation has to be used, it is important that all the storage is released; in complex cases some may not be, leading to creeping loss of storage.

25.4 Representation Clauses

Representation clauses are the principal way in which the language caters for interfacing to hardware devices and software systems. They specify how the types of the language are to be mapped to the underlying machine, and their use can achieve a more efficient packing of data items in structured data. For example, they may be used to control the amount of storage space allocated to an individual variable or the amount of working space available to a task. They may also be used to control the addresses within the target computer at which different items are to be located. Many questions can be asked about particular representation clauses if the application demands it. More general questions that can be asked are as follows.

Q25.4.1 What representation clauses are accepted by the compiler?

Q25.4.2 What restrictions apply to the various kinds of representation clause?

There is an extensive set of representation clauses in the language, and one language-defined representation pragma, PACK, which should cater for most interfacing situations, but the extent to which compilers support them is very variable and not, at the time of writing this Guide, well tested by the validation suite.

Q25.4.3 What conventions are used for names denoting implementation-defined components of a record?

Some implementations may include extra control or structuring information in records to make accessing more efficient. It is possible for a compiler to allow the application system developer to name such extra hidden fields in representation clauses; for example this would be useful when layout control of the record is required.

Q25.4.4 What is the interpretation of expressions that appear in address clauses?

The compilation system may be obliged to impose restrictions on what addresses may be specified as a result of the target architecture. For example, where there are separate address spaces for code and data controlled through base registers, it might reasonably be expected that the compilation system would interpret addresses for variables and constants as belonging to the data space, and addresses for subprograms, packages and task units as belonging to the code space. For a compilation system not to enforce this interpretation when perhaps it should do so might be considered a cause for concern.

Q25.4.5 Are there operations defined to manipulate addresses, remembering that ADDRESS may be a private or record type?

Address clauses allow the user to specify the address in the target computer where certain entities are stored. Other facilities for manipulating addresses may be supplied.

Q25.4.6 What is the effect of pragma PACK, especially where types whose size is less than 8 bits are involved?

This pragma requests the compiler to pack the elements of an array or record more closely than usual, that is to trade off access time for storage. The effectiveness of the pragma may be limited by the target hardware or by the compiler's handling of it.

Q25.4.7 Are interrupt entries supported?

Q25.4.8 Are there any other features implemented to speed up interrupt handling, for example special pragmas?

The basic facility for handling interrupts in Ada is by associating task entries with them by address clauses. Compilation systems can provide more advanced facilities.

25.5 Low-level Input-Output

Q25.5.1 Is LOW_LEVEL_IO provided and if so, what is its specification?

LOW_LEVEL_IO is a predefined package for control of attached devices. What, if any, devices and types of control the package supports is implementation-dependent.

Q25.5.2 Are there any other low-level input-output or machine control features provided, and if so, by what means?

LOW_LEVEL_IO is very general and may not be well suited to all situations. Other facilities may be provided by library packages or pragmas.

25.6 Implementation-Dependent Features

A compilation system may validly enhance the language by supporting certain implementation-defined pragmas and attributes.

Q25.6.1 What implementation-defined pragmas are provided, where are they allowed, and what are their effects?

Some pragmas may be specific to one compilation system and ignored, or even acted upon differently, when submitted to another. Such pragmas may also have effects on the object program. For example, a pragma MONITOR may mean, in one implementation, that a task is to be treated as a monitor task and implemented in a special way, but in another it might turn on compiler diagnostic output and generate reams of paper at compile time. The ISO Ada Working Group is trying to establish conventions to reduce the number of such cases, but they are unlikely ever to be eliminated entirely.

Q25.6.2 What are the names, forms, and effects of any implementation defined attributes provided by the system?

Unlike implementation-defined pragmas which if not recognised by an implementation must be ignored, an implementation-defined attribute which is not recognised by a compiler causes compilation to fail.

Q25.6.3 What are the implementation-defined characteristics of input-output?

Although standard input-output packages are defined by the language, many aspects are left to the implementation to define. For instance:

- the representation on the external medium of a file created by the predefined input-output packages;

- whether any control or structuring information is present in composite types written to the external file;

- limitations on, or special effects from the use of, language-defined pragmas.

Note that such pragmas may have run-time consequences in addition to affecting the compilation itself.

Q25.6.4 Are the pragmas SYSTEM_NAME, STORAGE_UNIT or MEMORY_SIZE supported?

Most compilers cannot sensibly implement these pragmas, and restrictions are allowed by the Reference Manual.

Q25.6.5 In what circumstances does pragma INLINE create extra dependences between compilation units?

Inlining a subprogram which has a separately-compiled body may mean that compilation units which call that subprogram have to be recompiled when the body of the subprogram is changed.

Language-Related Characteristics

Q25.6.6 In what circumstances are compile-time evaluable expressions which are not static expressions as defined in the Reference Manual evaluated using universal arithmetic?

In other words, does overflow of an intermediate result cause a run-time exception to be raised? For example, in

    A: constant INTEGER := 2**31-1;

the subexpression 2**31 causes integer overflow on a 32-bit machine; but the whole expression is in range and is accepted by some but not all compilation systems.

Q25.6.7 What are the implementation-defined characteristics of the compilation process?

The Reference Manual leaves these characteristics to the implementor as they have no effect on the meaning of any program written in the language, but they may have a significant effect on how the compilation system is implemented. That is, they may have effects on the cost of the compilation system and the efficiency of the compilation process. They can also affect the application system development process to the extent that they may have an impact on the amount of recompilation required as a result of changes to the source.

Examples of these characteristics are as follows:

- whether the bodies of generic units may be absent at the time of compiling an instantiation, and if so, whether they are instantiated when the bodies are compiled or at link time;

- in what circumstances extra dependences are created between the compilation units of a given program, for optimisation purposes. If any such dependences are created, recompiling one may force all the others to be recompiled;

- in what circumstances a generic declaration and its proper body are required to be part of the same compilation. An implementation may impose this restriction. One possible effect is to ensure that if the body of a generic is recompiled, its specification is also recompiled, thus forcing all units which instantiate it to be recompiled. This avoids some awkward implementation issues arising from the interaction of the separate compilation and generic instantiation mechanisms.

Q25.6.8 In what circumstances are the subunits of a generic unit required to be part of the same compilation as the body of the generic unit?

This is another possible restriction for simplifying the operation of a compilation system which may affect this manner of use in the development process.

26

Tool-Building Activities

26.1 Introduction

This questionnaire relates to the needs of users who wish to build their own software development tools, perhaps because no compilation system fully addresses their needs. This may be because of special host or target environments, particular development methods or project management styles, or for other reasons. It is not addressed to those whose main activity is writing such tools, though that is certainly an application for which Ada is suitable and the Guide as a whole covers many of the questions they need to ask.

26.2 Tool-building Interfaces

Q26.2.1 What tool-building interfaces are supported?

Not many compilation systems support extensive tool-building interfaces for outside use, since the costs of documentation and maintenance of such interfaces can be high, and the requirement for onward compatibility can be restrictive to development. An exception to this is Diana, which some compilation systems use as the internal representation of the parsed source code, and others may support as an external representation; it may be useful for some types of tools which are chiefly interested in syntactic aspects of Ada.

On the other hand, many compilation systems have internal interfaces which are useful for tool-building, and which the supplier might be willing to make available under certain conditions. Examples are internal representations of the source, symbol tables, debug tables, linker tables, flow graphs, and the like. Also public interfaces often exist which are not intended for tool building, but may be so used; these are principally rehosting and retargeting interfaces.

The rehosting interfaces are those required for transporting the compilation system to a different host; typically they are the interfaces between the compilation system and the operating system for access to source and object code and the program library, for invoking the compiler and other tools, for calling the native linker and loader, and for invoking operating system facilities such as storage management and reading the time.

The retargeting interfaces are those required for retargeting the system, that is converting it to support object programs running on a different target. They are of two kinds: compile-time interfaces between the target-dependent and target-independent parts of the system, and run-time interfaces between the target-independent parts of the run-time system and the generated code on one side and the run-time environment on the other.

All these interfaces should be isolated from the rest of the system, thoroughly documented as to both form and meaning, and under rigorous change control.

26.3 Reusable Components

Q26.3.1 Are there any identifiable reusable components of the compilation system?

As for tool-building interfaces, few compilation systems are yet constructed from components which are publicly available for reuse; but there may well be such components which can be made available under conditions. Examples are support packages for interfaces such as the symbol table; table-driven components such as lexical analysers, parsers, text formatters, and pattern matchers; and flow graph analysers.

26.4 Host Tools and Interfaces

Q26.4.1 What use does the compilation system make of host tools and interfaces?

Examples are host linkers and loaders, host editors, and operating system facilities such as filestore and storage management. Such uses lead to actually or potentially public interfaces which can be used for tool-building, where the compilation system itself does not provide the necessary facilities. For instance, if the program library is mapped on to the host filestore in a well defined way, other tools can access the program library via the host filestore, even though there is no public interface to the program library as such. Similarly the host linker may be able to provide information on the linking process of interest to a program analysis tool.

26.5 Development Tools

Q26.5.1 Are there any tools available which were used for development of the compilation system?

Such tools can range from specialised compiler-writer's tools, such as the parser generators used by almost every compiler development nowadays, to general tools of value in many applications. An example of the latter is a tool for translating data structure descriptions in abstract form into Ada support packages.

These development tools can be of great value in the construction of tools to be used with a compilation system. As they have been used in the construction of the compilation system they are compatible with it to a high degree; and they have achieved a certain degree of maturity through that use.

The tools may be generally available, proprietary to a third party, or proprietary to the supplier of the compilation system. In the last case they might not be commercially available, having been developed for in-house use only; the supplier however might still be willing to make them available.

27

Contractual Matters

27.1 Introduction

The topic of contractual matters is best considered using a model to describe the different agreements that can be present. In the simplest case a three tier model can be used which describes an Ada compilation system supplier, an application developer and an end-user. Typically there is a contract between the compilation system supplier and the application developer, and a separate contract between the application developer and the end-user. In certain cases, for example a training company, the second type of contract does not formally exist, although particular questions may still be relevant. It is also possible that there may be a number of contracts between one application developer and many end-users which all need to be satisfied.

The following questionnaire has been organised to reflect the items relevant to each type of contract. More complex models have not been used because they do not necessarily add to the questions which have to be addressed.

The validation process of an Ada compilation system is described in the Introduction to this Guide, however it is appropriate to first reiterate the important points:

- An Ada compilation system should not be termed such unless it has been through the validation process which is controlled by the AJPO and operated by establishments which are licensed by the AJPO.

- Once the compilation system has successfully completed the validation process a certificate is issued by the AJPO.

- A supplier can then make minor adjustments to the compilation system, at the supplier's discretion, but the compilation system must be revalidated if major changes are made, for example it is moved to a different operating system or new target.

- At the time of writing this Guide, the validation certificate expires twelve months after the relevant test suite has expired, and at this time the compilation system needs to be revalidated.

It is possible that the contractual requirements may not call for a compilation system which holds a validation certificate. This point and its implications must be positively addressed before it is accepted.

27.2 The Contract between the Application Developer and the End-User

27.2.1 Validation Policy

Q27.2.1.1 Is the validation certificate required and for what time period?

The question of the need for a validation certificate is addressed in the introduction. However the end-user may require only the purchased compilation system to have a validation certificate, as new issues of the compilation system are not relevant. An examples of this is a very short term project like a feasibility study to gain experience before project definition can begin.

27.3 The Contract between the Application Developer and the Compilation System Supplier

27.3.1 Validation Policy

Q27.3.1.1 Does the compilation system have a current validation certificate?

The compilation system validation certificate needs to be valid for the actual time of purchase, which may be some time after the date of enquiry. Therefore the expiry date for the certificate must be noted.

Q27.3.1.2 What is the validation policy of the compilation system supplier?

The compilation system needs to be revalidated once the current certificate has expired. If no modifications have been made, the compilation system supplier may be reluctant to apply for revalidation, even though a new test suite could be in operation. If the compilation system has been modified, all new versions need to be upwards compatible and validated. The importance of these points depends upon the period of the use of the compilation system.

Q27.3.1.3 What provisions have been made if a validation certificate is not going to be maintained?

If the compilation system supplier is not, for whatever reasons, going to guarantee that the validation certificate will be maintained for the lifetime of the project in question, then there are a number of actions the project can take. Firstly the source code and relevant documentation could be supplied so that the application developers can provide their own validation certificate, or subcontract the work to a third party. The compilation system supplier may be able to give the names of alternative suppliers who have given the necessary assurances. Finally the software may be lodged in escrow as a means of protecting its future viability. That is, copies of the source code and documentation may be deposited with a third party to be released to purchasers of the compilation system in the event that the supplier ceases trading or fails for some other reason to maintain the validated status of the compilation system.

27.3.2 Licence Policy

Q27.3.2.1 What type of usage can the compilation system be put to?

The compilation system supplier may have commercial, political or territorial reasons for restricting the use of the compilation system. This could involve restrictions on the use of the developed system, for instance non-military use only. Another example could be restrictions on how many users of the compilation system's host system there may be. A compilation system may also be on an approved list for use in particular applications, for example approved by military organisations, and this may also affect the licence agreement.

Q27.3.2.2 Is the licence giving the customer exclusive use?

This may not be a problem for the current purchaser when the exclusive rights are obtained but if a compilation system supplier exhibits a tendency to give exclusive rights to certain customers then it could inhibit the usefulness of the compilation system in the future. For example future updates may not be as widely available or new licence agreements will need to be negotiated with a different organisation which may impose unacceptable restrictions.

Q27.3.2.3 When does the licence expire?

The licence may only be valid for twelve months, for example, which could cause a risk to the project if a new agreement is required which proved to be unsatisfactory. However it may be that the licence is renewable which could be at extra cost.

Q27.3.2.4 Does the licence agreement include upgrades?

There are two types of upgrades possible although it is not common for them to be supplied separately. These are upgrades which correct faults and upgrades for improvements and enhancements. The cost of the licence may include updates free of charge, but it may be that a separate agreement is required in order to receive them.

Q27.3.2.5 Does the licence allow the further distribution the compilation system?

The application developer's project may require the inclusion of all or part of the compilation system in the product supplied to the end-user. The licence obtained from the compilation system supplier, as standard, may not include provisions for this distribution. It is most likely that the run-time system of the compilation system could be distributed with the application developer's product. However this is a frequent occurrence so it may well already be included in the licence agreement, but checks should be made. If the distribution of the compilation system is required in other forms, for example in source code or packages, a separate licence probably needs to be taken out.

27.3.3 Viability of the Compilation System Supplier

Q27.3.3.1 What is the financial status of the compilation system supplier?

If the project is other than short-term then the stability of the compilation system supplier is important. This does not only concern the possibility of required upgrades, but also affects validation status and the system support that can be offered. Some inferences can be made by examining annual reports of a compilation system supplier, especially if the examination can be made by a trained eye. It is also worth noting the clauses that are included in the contract to protect the application developer from the demise of the compilation system supplier.

Q27.3.3.2 What is the standing of the compilation system supplier in the Ada market?

Information about how well the compilation system has been received by bona fide customers is invaluable in assessing the viability of the compilation system supplier. This not only provides an indication of the acceptance of the compilation system, but also gives an insight into the market which has been reached. It may be that the compilation system is not necessarily suitable for the application in question if all the reports are from a different field.

27.3.4 The Availability of Different Targets

Q27.3.4.1 Are versions of the compilation system available from the supplier for a number of different targets, now and in the future?

The progression of the developed system, even once it has been delivered, may involve upgrading hardware to faster processors within the same family. In order to reduce the upgrade costs it could be proposed that the software is not, in general, altered. This is more easily achieved by obtaining a new compilation system from the same supplier assuming that upwards compatibility is specified. Although at first this may not seem necessary because an aim of the Ada language is portability, the implementation-dependent features may not aid portability between compilation systems from two different suppliers.

Q27.3.4.2 Are versions of the compilation system available from third party suppliers for a number of different targets, now and in the future?

This question has similar implications to the one above except that the agreement between the compilation system supplier and the third party must also be assessed. The supplier may act on behalf of the third party and market all the compilation systems which have the same front end regardless of the compilation system developer. Alternatively the compilation system supplier may be able to provide direct contact to the third party. The future of the third party agreement must be examined because it could be terminated, which would have a similar consequence as if one or other of the companies were to cease trading.

Q27.3.4.3 Is the compilation system supplier dependent on the tools of a third party?

The compilation system supplier may be developing a compilation system using software tools developed by a third party, for example a parser generator. The agreement between the compilation system supplier and the third party should contain guarantees of continued supply of the tool. If it does not, the compilation system supplier may have made other arrangements to protect the continued development of the compilation system.

Q27.3.4.4 Is information supplied which will allow the development of compilation systems for new targets?

The compilation system supplier may restrict to selected organisations the disclosure of the commercially valuable information needed to write a new code generator. If this information is available the interface needs to be guaranteed. That is it will remain upwards compatible so that as the front end is upgraded changes are not made to the interface which causes developed generators to cease functioning. How this information is supplied is also relevant as is the support and assistance given. Questions which relate to this are in Chapter 23, Architectural Considerations.

Q27.3.4.5 Is information supplied which will allow the development of tools which need access to internal compilation system interfaces?

This question is similar to the one above although the application field is different. The quality of the information supplied and the stability of the interface will influence the viability of the tool under development. Questions which relate to this are given in Chapter 26, Tool-Building Activities.

27.3.5 Installation and Maintenance Procedures

Q27.3.5.1 Does the licence agreement specify an installation policy?

The licence agreement may insist that the compilation system supplier installs the compilation system and any future upgrades there may be. This could cause an hidden unbudgeted cost. However installation of the compilation system could be sufficiently complex for an application developer to welcome the assistance of the supplier's staff.

Q27.3.5.2 Is the compilation system supplied on a medium that is suitable to the application developer?

If this is not true then the arrangements that can be made for the successful transfer of the compilation system to the required host need investigation. There may be copyright issues to be considered.

Q27.3.5.3 How many copies of the compilation system can be made?

There are two situations when the number of copies are important. Firstly backup copies of the host, and maybe the target, system are made for computer security reasons and these necessarily contain copies of the compilation system. The second situation is when there is a network of processors. It may be desirable to hold copies of the compilation system on each processor to optimise compile time. As the processors are linked by a network this configuration could be considered by the compilation system supplier as one system or many systems. The number of licence agreements could therefore be affected.

Q27.3.5.4 What support mechanisms are offered?

In the event of a problem about usage of the compilation system, the supplier needs to provide support. The level of the support, its location, how it is charged are all issues which are influences upon how efficiently the compilation system is utilised.

Q27.3.5.5 Is the installation of an upgrade mandatory for continued support?

An application developer may feel reluctant to install an upgrade to the compilation system because of the development cost this could impose, for example if it caused the recompilation of all the source code units. However the compilation system supplier may withdraw support to problems encountered with the previous version thus imposing restrictions on the application developer.

27.3.6 Performance Aspects

Q27.3.6.1 What is the status of performance information given in the literature provided before a sale?

If performance figures are provided then how they were derived is important when assessing which compilation system to purchase. The status of these figures is also relevant because if they are not in any way guaranteed then the application developer does not have any cause for recompense if they are not met. The legal enforceability of the statements in sales literature should be investigated.

Q27.3.6.2 What information may an application developer make public about the performance of a compilation system?

The compilation system supplier may impose restrictions about the publication of performance figures without their prior approval even after the compilation system has been purchased. The limitations may be particularly specified or there could be a total ban. The motives for the restrictions should be examined; the compilation system supplier could be publishing figures and so would not wish two sets of data available in the market place which could lead to confusion, or it could demonstrate a lack of self-confidence.

Q27.3.6.3 Are there any benchmarking figures available?

Standard benchmarks are continually being developed which examine different performance aspects of the compilation system. The compilation system supplier may have results available from the execution of a standard benchmark which can be used when comparing different compilation systems from the same or different suppliers.

PART III Sources of Information

28

Introduction to Part III

The previous chapters of this guide have surveyed the vital issues in the evaluation of an Ada compilation system. Part II of the guide has provided a series of questions whose individual relevance depends on the application area in question. However, the amount of information required to carry out an evaluation for anything other than a very specific application area is vast.

The amount of time required to collect the information needed to perform an evaluation can be greatly reduced if it is available in some standard and public way. The following chapters consider ways this information, together with some results from objective measurements of performance, can be supplied.

29

Benchmarks

29.1 Introduction

The purpose of a benchmark is to facilitate the comparative assessment of systems. In the context of computing, a system may be so wide as to involve all the hardware and both support and application software for some project, or it may be confined to a single component. For the purposes of this Guide, the system for which benchmarks are to be considered consists primarily of the Ada compilation system, but must also include, where appropriate, the support software and the machine or machines for which the compilation system is used. That is, the Guide is concerned with benchmarks of the compilation system in both the compilation and target execution environments.

29.2 General considerations

In connection with a compilation system a benchmark may be used to assess a number of different kinds of characteristic, such as compile-time performance, compiler limits, program library characteristics, code execution speed, and tasking performance.

It therefore follows that there can be no universal benchmark to suit all purposes and tastes. The benchmark user must decide what criteria are relevant to his assessment and construct or select a benchmark or set of benchmarks which will test or measure the various significant factors.

This is by no means a simple task if the use of the benchmarking process is really to select the most suitable product. It may still not be simple if the benchmark is being used to support a prejudice, which is by no means unknown. In addition the directly measurable factors must be balanced with many more subjective matters concerning usability, reliability, costs, and so on.

Having decided upon the bases of the benchmarking process the assessor must proceed to the selection or construction of a benchmark which will provide the required information. Such a benchmark may be a member of one of two classes: synthetic benchmarks and application benchmarks. These two classes have different characteristics and pitfalls, which are examined further in the following subsections. Synthetic benchmarks, particularly standard ones, can give generally comparable information quite quickly and cheaply, but unless used intelligently may give dangerously misleading results. On the other hand while a well designed application benchmark may give results which reflect the behaviour of the system with considerable accuracy, the cost is likely to be substantial.

29.3 Synthetic benchmarks

A synthetic benchmark is one consisting of a program or programs specially constructed to measure a particular set of characteristics of a computer system. It is not in itself and is not usually related to any really useful program; thus, for example, in a benchmark to measure disk subsystem performance, it is the quantity of data transferred which is important, and the data itself may not contain any information.

The advantage of a synthetic benchmark is that it may generate a simple numeric index giving some measure of conformity to a perceived ideal which permits a large range of products to be compared. Examples of such indices are:

- PIWG : a measure of run-time performance

- GAMM : a measure of floating point performance

- WHETSTONE : a measure of general scientific performance

Unfortunately this approach carries a number of serious pitfalls for the unwary.

The first difficulty is in interpreting the results and assessing the extent to which they are relevant to the system being considered.

The second, more subtle, problem concerns the extent to which such results, even where they are relevant, can be relied upon to reflect performance in a real situation. For example, when such indices are measured it is usually in an artificial state with an otherwise idle machine, when executing code in a real state with interactions with operating system and peripheral activity the relative performance of different machines may be very different.

Even worse, unless the benchmark is constructed very carefully, a highly optimising compiler may be able to defeat the benchmark's purpose, by recognising that certain code patterns are repeated, that calculated values are never really used or even by using particular special algorithms.

29.4 Application Benchmarks

An application benchmark is a program or set of programs selected or constructed to model the operational loading of a real application system. Thus, if well designed, such a benchmark will give a good indication of the performance of the computer in the intended application.

The nub of the problem with application benchmarks lies in the qualification "if well designed". The best benchmark for an application is the application itself and anything less than that must be both a simplification and an approximation to the real thing. Designing a benchmark which faithfully reproduces the performance characteristics of a large system while not involving excessive implementation costs is a very difficult undertaking.

30

Evaluation Systems

30.1 Introduction

The information required to make an evaluation of an Ada compilation system can be time consuming to collect. This chapter describes opportunities that may be available to the evaluator in order to make this task easier. During the lifetime of this Guide many more facilities may become available. If it is not possible to use any of these information services, and it should be remembered that they may provide far more information than can be easily assimilated, then the compilation system supplier should be able to give all the information necessary. The supplier may also be able to give results to performance tests that have been carried out independently.

Unfortunately, obtaining measurements from test programs is not easy. For performance tests, a dedicated machine is really needed, so that timing measurements will be repeatable. For tests of ease of use or assessing the helpfulness of the compiler error messages, guidance may be needed to make comparisons between systems meaningful. It is also essential that the tests are controlled properly in order to obtain correct and objective results.

The problems noted above of control and measurement are largely avoided if an independent test service is established rather like that for validation. The body performing the testing can then acquire the necessary expertise to avoid the pitfalls, for example to ensure that the test software has no obvious defects. Independent testing cannot usefully ignore the Ada compilation system supplier since some information can only be supplied by him.

30.2 The Ada Evaluation Service

The Ada Evaluation Service (AES) was established in 1987 by the UK Ministry of Defence (MOD) and is operated by the British Standards Institution (BSI). The service is available to any interested party with the necessary resources and authority to make the Ada compilation system in question available for evaluation.

At the time of writing this Guide, an evaluation report contains about 500 measurements taken by a suite of test programs, and the answers to a further 1000 or so questions, entered by the assessor. These are supplemented by notes and summaries by the assessor, and there is provision for comment on the report by the vendor.

The evaluation covers the compiler, linker, loader, debugger, run-time system and program library, and the aspects evaluated include compile-time and run-time performance and capacity, quality of information output, accuracy, error handling, usability, and functionality.

The layout of the report (which was completely revised in 1989) uses many devices to render accessible the large amount of information it contains. It is accompanied by a compendious reader's guide.

Commissioning a new evaluation is not cheap, as the process of evaluation takes several weeks of skilled effort. However, existing evaluation reports are generally available from BSI or the vendor at a reasonable price.

30.3   The Ada Compilation Evaluation Capability

The Ada Compiler Evaluation Capability (ACEC) was sponsored by the US Department of Defense (DoD); the first version became available in 1987. It is seen as a contribution to a Quality Testing Service, comparable to the AES, though at the time of writing this Guide the mode of operation of such a service is still under review.

The first version of the ACEC consists of about 1000 tests with support software to help run the tests and analyse the results. The tests evaluate the performance of an Ada compilation system in terms of execution speed, compilation speed, and code expansion size, and is thus more narrowly focused than the AES. A second version, due out at the end of 1989, adds more performance tests, extends the scope to include the program library system and debugger, and also assesses usability features and quality of error messages.

The structure and mode of use of the ACEC is modelled on the ACVC to some extent. A pre-evaluation period is required during which the client (usually the vendor) runs the ACEC suite and negotiates out inapplicable tests, after which the Ada Evaluation Facility performs the evaluation and publishes the report. User's and reader's guides are also available.

At the time of writing this Guide, export of the ACEC is controlled, and it is available outside the USA only via diplomatic channels. It is possible that this situation will be eased as the ACEC comes into use and Ada Evaluation Facilities are established.

31

Published Literature

This chapter describes what information is available in the public domain that is useful when selecting a compilation system. The details given here are relevant to the time of writing the Guide, and they are expected to be reasonably stable.

31.1 Lists of Validated Compilers

The Ada Joint Program Office (AJPO) maintains a list of all validated compilers which is updated every three months. This list identifies the host and target systems, the compiler supplier, the version of the validation test suite used during the validation and the expiry date of the validation certificate. It is the first reference point for identifying the compilation systems that are available for the particular software and hardware configuration to be used.

Apart from obtaining this list from the AJPO, it can also be obtained from the Ada Validation Facilities (AVFs) in France, West Germany, the United Kingdom and the United States of America. The addresses for the AVFs are given in the Glossary.

The list is also published in journals; for example Ada User, the journal of Ada Language UK Ltd (Ada UK), publishes the list from time to time.

31.2 Validation Summary Reports

Validation Summary Reports are produced at the time of validation. Their purpose is to document the results of the validation testing performed on an Ada compiler. The scope of the report is:

- to define the configuration of the system under test, including the host computer, the target computer, and their operating systems and memory sizes;

- to identify the implementation characteristics, for example capacities, rounding accuracy, the availability of certain predefined types and the facilities available for the compilation of generics;

- to identify dependences on the operating systems and hardware, as observed during the testing;

- to identify implementation strategies, as observed during the testing;

- to identify the implementation-dependent characteristics of the compiler discussed in Appendix F of the Reference Manual;

- to identify implementation dependent values, for example the largest integer available;

- to describe details of the test method used;

- to identify the tests that were determined as inapplicable and to give the reasons for categorising the tests as inapplicable;

- to identify the number of inapplicable, withdrawn and passed tests.

It is very unusual for the Validation Summary Report to be withdrawn from the public domain. Copies can usually be obtained from the compilation system supplier, the AVF that carried out the validation or the Ada Information Clearing House.

31.3 Ada-Europe Compilation Systems Conference Facility

The Ada-Europe Compilation Systems Assessment Working Group organises a conference on the Eurokom system whereby comments on different compilers can be made publicly available. The objective of the read-only conference is to provide a forum for publishing user comments about Ada compilation systems which may be useful to a potential user when making an assessment of the appropriateness of the system for a particular field of application.

It holds comments by actual users which have been acknowledged by the suppliers of the respective compilation systems. The conference is controlled by the National Computing Centre Ltd. The operating procedures are given below.

Comments uniquely identifying compilation system, release number, source of supply and the environment in which used, are submitted directly to the NCC Ltd. The suppliers of the Ada compilation system are then sent the comments, unedited and with the author's names, and are requested to respond. As responses are received, the comments, the names of the authors of the comments and the responses are added to the conference.

Glossary

Ada Information Clearinghouse:
Provides copies of the Validation Summary Reports in the public domain.
    Address: AJPO
                       OUSDRE
                       The Pentagon
                       Rm 3D-139 (Fern Street)
                       Washington DC
                       20301-3081

AVF:
The Ada Validation Facility. The AVF is responsible for conducting compiler validations according to procedures contained in the Ada Compiler Validation Procedures and Guidelines (AJPO 1987). The addresses for the different AVFs are:

    France: AFNOR
                      Tour Europe
                      cedex 7
                      F-92080 Paris la Defense

    W.Germany: Industieanlagen-
                      Betriebsgesellschaft mbH
                      Dept. SZT (IABG-AVF)
                      Einsteinstrasse 20
                      D-8012 Ottobrunn

    UK: The NCC Ltd
                      Oxford Road
                      Manchester
                      M1 7ED

    USA: Language Control facility
                      ADS/ADOL
                      Wright-Patterson AFB
                      OH 45433

and Institute for Computer Science Technology (ICST) National Bureau of Standards Building 225 Room A266 Gaithersburg MD 20899-9999

Deadly Embrace:
A deadlock situation where two or more parallel processes each requires a resource held by one of the other processes before it can continue.

Diana:
A Descriptive Intermediate Attributed Notation for Ada, designed as a means of representing Ada code internally within a compiler; it was intended to be particularly suitable for communication between the front and back ends of an Ada compiler, and also for use with other tools in an Ada programming environment.

Direct Memory Access (DMA):
A hardware mechanism whereby a transfer of a block of data into or out of main storage, once initiated, can proceed without program intervention.

Dongle:
A protected hardware device accessible by program and containing coded information such that the program will refuse to function correctly without the presence of the properly coded device.

Garbage Collector:
Part of a storage management mechanism which detects areas of storage which are no longer being used (or usable) by a program and returns them to a pool of available storage for reallocation.

In-lining:
A code optimization technique whereby the code calling a subprogram is replaced by the parameterised code of the subprogram itself.

MASCOT:
Modular Approach to Software Construction, Operation and Test - a method for expressing the software structure of a real-time system, together with the means for constructing such a system.

Partial Linking:
A technique whereby a consistent subset of compiled modules of a program is linked together to form a unit which may be used as though

it were an individual component in subsequent linking operations. Partial linking may be used to remove the need for relinking a fully tested subsystem whenever it has to be linked with other components.

Pretty Printer:
A tool which prints program or data in a defined format, irrespective of the format in which it is presented.

Public Tool Interface:
An interface at the program level with a stable, published definition designed to permit tools written by other parties to interact with the data and processes of the system.

RAM:
The main working storage of a computer, (originally Random Access Memory).

ROM:
Read Only Memory - Part of the main storage of a computer with contents that cannot be changed by program.

SSADM:
The Structured Analysis and Design Method - the standard UK government method for analysis and design of computer systems.

Variant:
An instance of an item defined to satisfy a particular requirement. When several conflicting requirements must be met, variants which represent functional differences within the item will be established and these may be developed concurrently.

Version:
An instance of an item or a variant created at a particular time. Successive versions represent progressions in time.

References

Ada-Europe Formal Methods Working Group. Forthcoming Guide to Verifiable Ada.

AJPO. Ada Compiler Validation Procedures and Guidelines 1 January 1987

B.A.Carré and T.J.Jennings. SPARK - The SPADE Ada Kernel vs 1.0. University of Southampton. March 1988

DoD Computer Security Center. Trusted Computer System Evaluation Criteria, CSC-STD-001-83. Department of Defense. 15 August 1983

Joint IECCA and MUF Committee. The Official Handbook of MASCOT Version 3.1 RSRE Malvern UK, June 1987

T.G.L.Lyons and J.C.D.Nissen (editors). Selecting an Ada Environment. CUP Ada Companion Series.

J.C.D.Nissen and P.J.L.Wallis (editors). Portability and Style in Ada. CUP Ada Companion Series.

Reference Manual for the Ada Programming Language, ANSI/MIL-STD 1815A. January 1983.

PCTE - a basis for a Portable Common Tool Environment. Fifth edition.

M.W.Rogers (editor). Ada: languages, compilers, and bibliography. CUP Ada Companion Series.

ACM SIGAda Numerics Working Group. Proposed ISO standard for elementary functions in Ada.

PIWG. Refer to SIGAda Performance Issues Working Group. Chairman listed in Ada Letters, SIGAda. 1987.

A.A.Hook et al. User's Manual for the Prototype Ada Evaluation Capability (ACEC). Version 1. Technical Report P-1879. Institute for Defence Analyses, October 1985.

The Ada Evaluation Service (AES). BSI-QA. December 1987. (Tele +44 908 220908).

References

B.A.Wichmann. Validation code for the Whetstone benchmark, NPL Report DITC 107/88. 1988.

INDEX

Access Control Mode 71
Accreditation 80
Ada Joint Program Office 1
Address ix, 1, 8, 12, 21, 23, 43-45, 47, 48, 62, 74, 75, 80, 109,
    112, 113, 114, 116, 118
  Clause 75, 114
  Space 12, 44, 47, 62, 114, 118
AJPO 1, 2
Architecture 18, 33, 44, 45, 48-50, 53, 74, 75, 103, 111, 113, 116,
    121
Array Processor 32, 53, 55
ASCII 104, 106
Asynchronous
  Task 116
Backing Storage 29, 47
Backup 90
Baseline 11, 71, 72
Benchmark v, 2, 91, 94, 96
Build 11, 71, 72, 81, 108
Capacity v, 8, 15, 16, 22, 49, 59, 86, 91, 92, 116
  Limit 59
Character Set 1, 24, 104-106
Classified Information 71
Coding Standard 10, 76, 77
Common Utility 70
Communication
  Inter-task 33, 116
  Intra-program 99
Compatibility viii, 9, 10, 13, 14, 24, 50, 52, 59, 60, 112, 113
Compilation Unit 35, 92, 93
Compile Time v, 8, 15, 85, 88, 91, 92, 94, 98, 100
Component 8, 11, 19-23, 26, 43-45, 53, 54, 86, 113, 116, 119,
    120
Concurrency v, 8, 31, 32
Configuration
  Control 11, 71, 72, 114
Covert Channels 35
Cross-reference Lister 10, 17, 77
Crossloading 41
Customer Base 79
Deadly Embrace 31
Debugger 2, 16, 18, 62, 73, 74, 96, 105

Debugging vii, 10, 18, 41, 69, 74, 94, 104, 105
  Facility 69, 74
  Interactive vii, 41
Design Methodology 62
Development
  Environment 18, 69, 72, 91, 95
  Method 20, 41, 69, 72, 83
  Team 15, 84, 86
Device Driver 29, 118
Diana 36
Discretionary Access Control 35, 71
Distributed System 22, 37, 51, 52, 56
Documentation v, vii, 1, 10, 11, 17-19, 28, 38, 59-63, 71, 77, 79, 85, 88, 95, 100, 104-107, 109
Downloading 41
Dynamic Reconfiguration 120
Dynamically Allocated Variable 27, 38
EBCDIC 104
Editor ix, 2, 16, 17, 69, 73, 77
  Syntax-driven 73
Embedded System 1, 8, 44, 63, 103
Environment 2, 9, 13, 14, 18, 19, 23, 25, 28, 29, 31, 38, 41, 45, 47, 50, 61-63, 69, 72, 82, 86, 91, 95, 98, 100, 103-105, 116, 120
Error
  Report 19
Exception 18, 25, 28, 48, 73, 88, 89, 93, 97, 101, 121
  Handling 25, 28, 101
Floating Point 21, 49, 50, 75, 107
  Processor 50, 75
Formatter 17, 77
Garbage Collector 27, 37, 38, 97, 99, 122
Generated Code 25, 26, 37, 60, 92, 95, 96, 98
Generic Instantiation 92
Host 14, 108, 109, 123
Host-target v, 8, 18, 41, 74, 103, 105, 123
Icons 19
Identifier 106
Implementation Defined 89
Implementation Dependent 62, 84
In-circuit emulator 38, 41
Instruction Set 50
Integration 11, 15, 19, 20
Integrity viii, 11, 20, 35, 36, 89, 90
Interrupt 27, 29, 37-39, 43, 44, 47, 48, 70, 89, 101

Index

Large Program Size v, 8, 11
Licensing Agreement 63
Lifetime v, 8-10, 44, 69, 91, 108
Linker 2, 17, 45, 62, 75, 94, 95
Listing 2, 17, 36, 62, 94
 Tool 2, 17
Local Area Network 52
Loosely Coupled 52-54, 56
Machine Code 22, 23, 39, 43, 47, 49, 120
Maintainability 9, 10
Maintenance 8-10, 14, 18, 36, 54, 61, 63, 76, 77, 80, 81, 90, 108, 111
 Agreement 81
Man-machine Interface v, 69, 73, 86
Mandatory Access Control 35, 71
MASCOT 59, 72, 83, 100
Mathematical Library 86
Maturity 2, 10, 80-83
Menus 19
Monitor Routine 118
Multiprocessing v, 51
Multiprocessor 31, 32, 52, 53, 56, 75, 100, 113
Multitasking 50
Nested Tasks 93, 96, 101
Object Oriented Design 83
Operating System 2, 9, 14, 21, 23, 24, 29, 36, 53-55, 61, 69, 79, 84, 87-89, 100, 116-118, 121, 122
Optimisation 21, 92
Orange Book 87
Overload 38, 101
Package 12, 23, 29, 35, 47, 49, 86, 93, 96, 100, 101, 104, 114
Parallel Execution 26, 27, 31-33, 39, 44, 53-56, 71, 113
Parameter 17, 21, 29, 50, 61, 85, 93
Partial
 Linking 11, 17, 70, 94
 Loading 86
Performance v, 15, 16, 18, 25-27, 33, 37, 38, 45, 54, 74, 75, 84, 86, 91, 92, 94, 95, 108, 110, 112
Portability v, vii, viii, 10, 13, 14, 76, 84, 103, 108, 109
Pragma 22, 76, 101, 114
Pre-sale Literature 79
Pretty Printers 17
Procedure 11, 14, 21, 27, 56, 59, 75, 76, 100, 115

Program Library vii, 10, 11, 18, 19, 22, 23, 49, 56, 69-72, 77, 86, 87, 89, 90, 93, 96, 109, 119-123
 Manager 18, 19, 77
Programmable Logic Analysers 41
Project Support Environment 61, 62
Quality Indicator 79
Real-time Clock 39, 44, 100
Recompilation 10-13, 50, 94, 95, 114, 119
Redundancy 51, 54, 55
Reference Manual vii, 1, 11, 17-19, 28, 62, 88, 100, 104-107
Regression Testing 81
Reliability 15, 16, 83, 118, 119
Remote Procedure Call 56, 75, 115
Rendezvous 28, 33, 75, 97, 101
Response Time 26, 37, 38, 43, 62
Reuse 11
Robustness 15, 16, 25, 29, 82, 83, 99
Run Time v, vii, 8, 12, 15, 22-29, 33, 35, 37-39, 43, 50, 53-55, 62, 63, 74, 75, 84, 85, 88, 89, 91, 95-101, 114, 115, 116-118, 120-123
 Support Software 26, 117, 121, 122
Scheduling 25, 27, 28, 31-33, 38, 39, 44, 50, 53, 56, 97, 98, 101, 116, 117
Secrecy 35, 36
Security v, viii, 35, 36, 51, 52, 56, 71, 87
 Rating 36, 71, 87
Serialisation 31, 32
Shared
 Data 75, 122, 123
 Libraries 120, 123
Source Code Generators 62
SSADM 59
Standard Package 95
Standby
 Facility 51, 55
 System 54
Static Checking 94
Storage
 Allocation 97
 Capacity 16
 Mapping 114
 Space 26, 101
Synchronisation 31, 32, 53, 116

Index

System
  Clock 50
  Error 88
  Usage Statistics 62
Target 14, 38, 41
  Bare 72, 116-118
  Computer 26, 50, 72, 73
  Loader 2, 18, 45, 96, 114
  Simulator 123
Task Scheduler 33
Tasking 18, 23, 25-28, 32, 33, 35, 38, 39, 44, 47, 50, 51, 53, 55, 56, 59, 61, 69, 73, 76, 91, 93, 96, 97, 99-101, 113-117, 121, 123
Tightly Coupled 52, 53, 55
Timing v, 8, 37, 38, 43, 50, 96, 97
Training v, 8, 61-63
Transaction Mechanism 90
Unauthorised Access 8, 35, 87
User
  Documentation 85
  Group 71
  Interface 19, 20, 63, 123
Validation vii, 1, 2, 9, 17, 69, 80, 81, 84, 105, 122
  Authority 80
  Certificate 2, 80
  Facility 84
  Status 122
  Summary Report 17, 84
  Test Suite 1, 2, 69, 80, 81, 84
Variant 13, 19, 21, 70-72, 76, 77, 106, 108, 110, 114, 120
Verification 10, 35
Version 9-12, 22, 24, 70-72, 76, 77, 81, 82, 90, 96, 114, 119, 120
Word Length 52

FEB 4 1991